FORTS & BATTLEFIELDS

OF THE OLD WEST

FORTS & BATTLEFIELDS
OF THE OLD WEST

PHOTOGRAPHS BY LYNN RADEKA

TEXT BY LINDOR REYNOLDS

MALLARD
PRESS

An imprint of BDD Promotional Book Company, Inc.,
666 Fifth Avenue, New York, New York 10103

(*Previous pages*) Presidio La Bahia, Goliad, Texas.

An imprint of BDD Promotional Book Company, Inc., 666 Fifth Avenue, New York, New York 10103

ISBN 0-7924-5215-1

AN M&M BOOK
Forts and Battlefields of the Old West was prepared and produced by M & M Books; 11 W. 19th Street, New York, New York 10011.

Project Director & Editor Gary Fishgall
Editorial Assistants Maxine Dormer, Ben D'Amprisi, Jr., Mitchell Weisberg, Ben McLaughlin; *Copyediting* Keith Walsh; *Proofreading* Shirley Vierheller.
Designer Binns and Lubin / Martin Lubin
Separations and Printing Regent Publishing Services Ltd.

Contents

INTRODUCTION 6

The Great Plains and Rocky Mountains

FORT SCOTT 10
FORT SCOTT, KANSAS

FORT ROBINSON 18
CRAWFORD, NEBRASKA

WOUNDED KNEE BATTLEFIELD 24
PINE RIDGE, SOUTH DAKOTA

FORT MEADE 28
STURGIS, SOUTH DAKOTA

FORT SISSETON 34
LAKE CITY, SOUTH DAKOTA

FORT TOTTEN 40
FORT TOTTEN, NORTH DAKOTA

FORT UNION 46
WILLISTON, NORTH DAKOTA

BENT'S OLD FORT 54
LA JUNTA, COLORADO

The Northwest

FORT LARAMIE 62
FORT LARAMIE, WYOMING

FORT BRIDGER 68
FORT BRIDGER, WYOMING

CUSTER BATTLEFIELD 76
CROW AGENCY, MONTANA

**BIG HOLE
BATTLEFIELD 82**
WISDOM, MONTANA

**FORT HALL
RECREATION 88**
POCATELLO, IDAHO

FORT CLATSOP 94
ASTORIA, OREGON

FORT NISQUALLY 98
TACOMA, WASHINGTON

FORT VANCOUVER 106
VANCOUVER, WASHINGTON

The Southwest

THE ALAMO 114
SAN ANTONIO, TEXAS

PRESIDIO LA BAHIA 120
GOLIAD, TEXAS

**SAN JACINTO
BATTLEFIELD 126**
HOUSTON, TEXAS

FORT DAVIS 132
FORT DAVIS, TEXAS

FORT SELDEN 140
LAS CRUCES, NEW MEXICO

FORT HUACHUCA 144
SERRE VISTA, ARIZONA

The Far West

COVE FORT 152
COVE FORT, UTAH

FORT ROSS 158
JENNER, CALIFORNIA

SUTTER'S FORT 162
SACRAMENTO, CALIFORNIA

FORT TEJON 170
BAKERSFIELD, CALIFORNIA

CREDITS AND ACKNOWLEDGEMENTS 176

INTRODUCTION

The history of the Old West is grander, bloodier, and more dramatic than anything Hollywood could ever devise. Few of the countless Westerns made since the earliest silent era truly depicted the hardships encountered by the brave men and women who settled the American frontier, by the soldiers who defended them and the land, and by the Native Americans who were often brutalized by the white intruders.

As the settlement of the lands west of the Mississippi progressed, so too did the establishment of secure forts throughout the region. The reasons for their construction varied widely and were not always related to warfare. The fur trade, for example, gave rise to many of the posts, as both trappers and traders required places to conduct commerce. Other forts were established to meet the needs of the pioneers making the long trek from Missouri to the "Promised Land" by covered wagon. Of course, some forts *were* military, used as bases for soldiers garrisoned to protect settlers from attacks by Mexicans or Indians or both.

Some posts served a multitude of purposes, adapting over the years to the changing requirements of the area. In time, some even found themselves serving civilian functions, acting as a school in one instance covered in this volume. Others were abandoned. A few, remarkably, continue to serve as active military installations to this day.

We typically think of western forts as American in character, but a number of them, including Fort Vancouver, were owned by British companies. Even more surprisingly, California's Fort Ross was built as a settlement for Russian and Alaskan fur traders. Its

(opposite) One of the most distinctive outposts of the Old West was Fort Ross, established in 1812 in what is now Jenner, California, by the Russian American Company.

walled enclosure lent itself easily to defense; it even boasted a grand looking cannon. Nevertheless, there was never a shot fired in anger at Fort Ross, which served solely as the basis for the Tsar's largely unrealized aspirations for New World territory.

Utah's Cove Fort was established by Latter-Day Saints who wanted to help fellow members settle in an area known as the "Mormon Corridor," which stretched from Utah to California. The fort provided living quarters for permanent and temporary residents and a place to feed and rest animals. It also acted as a relay station for the Deseret Telegraph.

Fort Bridger incorporates much of the West's frontier history. When people think of pioneer forts, they're likely to picture something like this Wyoming post. Built by mountain man Jim Bridger as a trading post, it originally consisted of a series of rough log buildings. It was later rebuilt and occupied by the army, which added 29 structures. Later still, the fort served in turn as a way station for the Pony Express and the Overland stagecoach, as a base for volunteer regiments, and as a supply station for regular troops in the western part of the Wyoming territory.

Some forts saw little or no action during their nonetheless distinguished histories, but others witnessed terrible brutalities and carnage. Among the latter, few are better remembered than the Alamo, one of the world's most famous battle sites. This former Spanish mission became the scene of an unforgettable engagement on March 6, 1836, when Mexican general Antonio Lopez de Santa Anna, accompanied by 3,000 men, attacked and killed 189 of the fort's defenders. The rebels' valiant stand at the Alamo was to become both a symbol and an inspiration to the Texans in their battle for independence.

Other forts serve as reminders of the shameful treatment dealt to Native Americans by whites during the 19th century. North Dakota's Fort Totten,

for example, was constructed to carry out agreements between the federal government and the tribes of the area. These agreements, which were common throughout the West, often robbed natives of their land and relegated them to reservations. The post was decommissioned in 1880 and it became an Indian industrial school. Its mission thereafter was to "civilize" native children. But the sad reality was that most of the youngsters who came of age there simply lost their heritage and found themselves unwelcome in a white man's world.

Settling the Old West was not easy. Even today the landscape is dotted with battlefields where opposing forces—white and Indian, Mexican and American—clashed. Wounded Knee, Big Hole, and San Jacinto are just a few of the battlesites that have been preserved, thanks largely to the efforts of dedicated volunteers.

Recalling the myriad forts and battlefields of the Old West as they were in the 19th century and as they are today is what this book is all about. To capture 26 sites in contemporary color images, photographer Lynn Radeka traveled almost half the nation. His journeys re-created many of the paths of the pioneers, as he moved from the West (stopping in Colorado, Kansas, Nebraska, and South Dakota), to the Northwest (as far as Oregon and Washington) to the Southwest (with visits to Arizona, Texas, and New Mexico) and finally to the Pacific coast and his native state of California. His photographs capture the spirit of these forts and battlefields and through them the men and women who helped tame a wilderness. Hopefully, these pictures, together with the histories of the sites and an array of vintage imagery, will serve to honor our fallen heroes, help us savor our victories, and remind us of our defeats. It is a journey worth the taking because a vibrant and colorful part of our national past lies in the remains of these Old West landmarks.

The Great Plains and Rocky Mountains

(*above*) The magazine, used to house the fort's explosives, powder, cartridges, fuses, and primers, is situated in the middle of the parade ground.

(*opposite*) An antique cannon sits beside the Wilson-Goodlander house, first built in 1845 as quarters for officers and their families and later used as a private residence.

(*previous pages*) The parade ground at Fort Sisseton in northeastern South Dakota.

During the first half of the 19th century, the federal government was determined to restrict the Indian tribes to certain designated portions of the country. The Removal Act of 1830 was a bold step in the implementation of this policy. It established a boundary between the lands owned by Native Americans and those open to white settlement and forced the tribes living east of that line to leave their homes and travel to what is now Kansas, Nebraska, and Oklahoma, a journey that one tribe—the Cherokee—called the "Trail of Tears."

To insure the cultural division of the country, the government established outposts in what was then designated Indian territory. Among those installations was Fort Scott, constructed in 1842. Strategically located between Fort Leavenworth in what is northeastern Kansas today and Fort Gibson, 150 miles to the south (northern Oklahoma today), it was part of a chain of army posts stretching from Minnesota to Louisiana. These forts were manned by infantry and by dragoons, a special breed of mounted, colorfully dressed, and heavily armed soldiers trained to fight on foot as well as on horseback.

Fort Scott was named for Gen. Winfield Scott, a major general of the army and later a hero of the Mexican War.

Fort Scott was on the ancestral land of the Osage, the dominant tribe of the region. Although they were known as good warriors and hunters, the natives posed little military threat. By the time of the army's occupation, the tribe had been relocated to a reservation southwest of the fort. Its relations with the army were primarily peaceful. Indeed, the tribal members often came to the fort to trade and the dragoons frequently rode onto their land to evict squatters.

In 1842, two companies of U.S. Dragoons—approximately 130 troopers—arrived at the site and began putting up the first quarters. They did most of the building themselves, aided only by a few skilled craftsmen. They used the raw materials that grew nearby—walnut, ash, and oak—supplemented by stone from the surrounding hills. The new post was named for Gen. Winfield

When they weren't escorting caravans along the Santa Fe Trail or conducting expeditions far into Indian country, the dragoons settled into the routine of garrison life, which included daily drills.

Bleeding Kansas

During the 1850s, as the United States teetered on the brink of civil war, a fragile balance of power existed in Congress between the free states and the slave states. Into that powder keg were tossed the territories of Kansas and Nebraska, allowed by act of Congress to decide by popular sovereignty if they would permit slavery in their territories or not. It was almost a foregone conclusion that Nebraska would become a free state. Thus, Kansas had to accept slavery if the precious balance of power were to be preserved. Instead, the territory became the prize in a tug of war between North and South. It was a contest that began with political corruption and ended in shocking displays of violence.

The contest started innocuously enough, with a group of abolitionists in New England. Led by Eli Thayer and industrialist Amos Lawrence, they formed the New England Aid Company to raise $5 million and send 20,000 free-land advocates to Kansas. That, they believed, would be sufficient to seize the territory's political machine. In 1854, the society did manage to send about 700 settlers, where they formed the antislavery town of Lawrence, but New England was really too far away to become a dominant force in Kansas' political life.

The pro-slavery forces, meanwhile, had their own plan. When the election to choose the territory's delegate to Congress was held in fall 1854, they arranged for slave owners to travel across the Missouri border into Kansas, vote, and return home. Consequently, of the 2,871 ballots counted, at least half were probably fraudulent. The winner, to no one's surprise, was John Whitfield, a proslavery candidate.

The conflict between the two camps turned physical in 1856, when the town of Lawrence was pillaged by Southern guerrillas. Abolitionist John Brown, his sons, and supporters retaliated by dragging five proslavery men from their isolated cabins, mutilating and killing them. Proslavery forces then attempted to capture Brown, who managed instead to trap his enemies. All that summer, the strife continued as ruffians from both sides murdered an estimated 200 people, burned crops, and destroyed property. "Bleeding Kansas" became the sad but accurate nickname for the territory.

Kansas eventually entered the union—as a free state in 1861—but by then the dress rehearsal for war that had taken place in the territory no longer seemed consequential. The nation was in the midst of the bloodiest conflict in its history.

A peace convention at Fort Scott erupts into conflict, typical of the intense feelings that gave rise to the nickname Bloody Kansas.

Scott, a major general of the army and later a hero of the Mexican War. Standing on a bluff surrounded by prairie and gently rolling hills, it was planned around a spacious parade-ground, with officers' quarters lining one side and dragoon barracks and stables on another. Post quartermaster Capt. Thomas Swords directed the erection of a hospital, a magazine, storehouses, and the support buildings required by an isolated post. Most of these structures were complete by 1848 and construction stopped entirely in 1850 when men, money, and materials ceased to be available.

Although the fort's garrison was primarily intended to serve as a peace-keeping force between the relocated Indians, the white settlers, and various nomadic tribes, violent outbreaks among the disparate cultures were rare. The dragoons frequently escorted caravans along the Santa Fe Trail and conducted expeditions far into Indian country. In 1844, for example, dragoons from both Fort Scott and Fort Leavenworth participated in an expedition into Pawnee country in an attempt to end the fighting between that tribe and the Sioux.

In 1845, Stephen Watts Kearny, a frontier veteran and commander of the dragoons, led his horse soldiers 2,200 miles in 99 days, deep into the land of the Plains Indians. This well-planned march took the troops up the Platte River to Fort Laramie and beyond, down the Rockies to the Arkansas River, and back home along the Santa Fe Trail. This trek proved the versatility of the dragoons and gave Kearny the chance to guard emigrants along the Oregon Trail, establish contact with the Sioux and Cheyenne tribes, and make useful geographical sightings.

Life for the men of Fort Scott varied between the excitement and adventure of a journey such as Kearny's to the monotony of everyday garrison duty. The dragoons were drilled almost daily in horsemanship and the art of soldiering. In one frequently practiced drill called "running at the heads," dragoons on horseback used both pistol and

(above) The quartermaster's storehouse contained everything that was needed to put a fighting force into the field. All of the troopers' supplies—from bullets to uniforms—were issued from this building.

At Fort Scott, the dragoons worked their own gardens, planting such items as corn, beans, potatoes, and squash. By providing themselves with fresh vegetables, they managed to avoid the scurvy that had caused fatalities at another fort in the region.

Laundresses were paid by the army to clean the men's clothes. For this service, each soldier contributed 50 cents per month from his $8 paycheck. During Fort Scott's heyday, there were probably about 12 laundresses on the post.

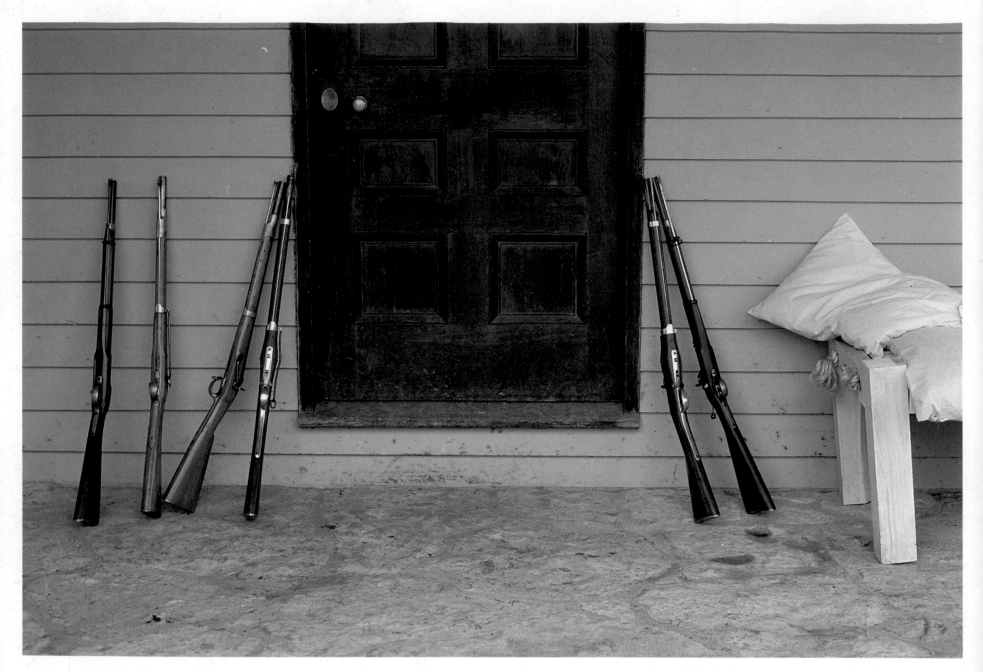

saber while charging at dummy heads mounted on posts. If the dragoons could, at least, relieve the monotony of barracks life with the occasional escort duty or expedition, the infantrymen found their tour at Fort Scott reduced to a mixture of guard duty, drills, construction, and maintenance.

This life came to an end in 1853, when the Indian policy was changed to reflect new concerns over westward expansion. Fort Scott was abandoned and the garrison transferred to Fort Leavenworth. Troops returned to the fort in 1857, however, and again in 1858 to quell civilian unrest caused by the larger national controversy over slavery. Fighting along the Missouri–Kansas border grew so fierce that the

territory became known as "Bleeding Kansas." During the Civil War, the U.S. Army returned in large numbers and the fort served as the headquarters of the Army of the Frontier, as a supply depot, training base, and refugee center for displaced Indians, escaped slaves, and settlers who were uprooted by the conflict. Fort Scott was also home of the First Kansas Colored Volunteer Infantry Regiment, which was the first African-American regiment to enter the U.S. Army from a northern state during the Civil War.

Today, Fort Scott National Historic Site, 90 miles south of present-day Kansas City, consists of 18 buildings that have been restored and reconstructed and is administered by the National Park Service. Throughout the

summer months, the frontier garrison life of an 1840s military fort is depicted through living history demonstrations, guided tours, and related interpretive programs. On specific weekends in spring and fall, visitors can enjoy the annual Civil War Encampment, Mexican War Encampment, or an American Indian celebration.

FORT ROBINSON

CRAWFORD, NEBRASKA

(above) The distant cabin in this photo is the place where Crazy Horse, victor of the Battle of the Little Big Horn, met his death. The noted Sioux chief, lured to the site on the pretext of settling a dispute, was bayoneted in the abdomen.

(opposite) Fort Robinson's blacksmith shop was built in 1904 to serve the needs of the 500–600 mounted soldiers stationed on the post. A second smithy, built two years later, subsequently became a harness repair shop.

The history of Fort Robinson is a colorful one, encompassing the bloody struggle for the great American Prairie that took place between the whites and Native Americans during the 19th century.

The fort's origins can be traced to the early 1840s, when the federal government sought to pave the way for settlement in the Platte Valley of Nebraska and eastern Wyoming. Although negotiations were conducted with the indigenous people of the area and some recompense was attempted, conflicts between whites and Indians could not be averted. By 1864, the Platte Valley was aflame with war, as settlers and those passing through the region on the trek to the far West endured constant fear of Indian attack. In the hopes of ending the bloodshed, peace commissioners appointed by President Andrew Johnson met at Fort Laramie with the Sioux chiefs in 1866. A key figure in the negotiations was Red Cloud, a Sioux Indian born near Nebraska's Platte River in 1822. He had distinguished himself as a warrior, both against the U.S. Army and his more traditional enemies, the Crows. The peace conference failed, due in large part to Red Cloud's eloquent speeches,

19

and warfare continued. Finally, a treaty was signed in 1868, creating an Indian reservation and enabling the Indians to retain certain hunting privileges. In 1870, a final settlement was reached. Among its terms was the establishment of the Red Cloud Agency in northwest Nebraska, a distribution site for rations, and annuities for the Native Americans. It soon became as well the focal point for Indian grievances, and a symbol of conquest for thousands of Sioux, Cheyenne, and Arapaho.

The Red Cloud Agency housed a number of Indians, who exercised their treaty right to hunt on the unceded land. Others lived there nomadically in the summer months. Until its removal to South Dakota in 1877, the agency requisitioned up to 8,000 daily rations per year. The winter issues were significantly higher.

Despite the treaty, hostility between natives and the government had been growing and it was felt a strong military presence in the area was needed to preserve the peace. To that end, 547 cavalrymen left Fort Laramie for the Red Cloud Agency in March 1874. Two days later, 402 infantrymen joined them and a tent camp was established near the agency blockhouse. The army named its group of tents Camp Robinson, in honor of Lt. Levi Robinson, killed the previous month. In effect, the Red Cloud Agency became part of Camp (later Fort) Robinson. It would remain on the site for three more years.

Concern over Indian hostilities proved justified and after skirmishes with the Indians erupted at Red Cloud, the tent camp was relocated for safety to a site about one-and-a-half miles away. Camp Robinson's first year was a tense one, with the possibility of a bloody war always looming. The Sioux representative, Red Cloud, figured highly in the peacekeeping operations.

Despite the army's efforts to move the Indians onto permanent reservations, battles between whites and Indians continued. Finally in 1873, the natives were relocated 75 miles away to the new Red Cloud Agency. By 1877, for the first time in its existence, Camp Robinson had no Indian camps in its immediate vicinity. The soldiers settled into the dull routine of garrison life, unaware that one of the bloodiest and (opposite) The officers' quarters are now used to house visitors to Fort Robinson, the largest state park in Nebraska.

The post's second blacksmith shop, built in 1906, became a harness repair shop during World War II.

The Demise of the Buffalo

The near destruction of Indian civilization during the 19th-century was not solely as a result of combat with whites; it can be attributed as well to the whites' wholesale slaughter of the buffalo. For generations, the Indians had used the huge animals—technically, bison—for an amazing variety of purposes. When the buffalo disappeared, an entire way of life vanished as well.

The buffalo once numbered in the millions. They were enormous, with an adult male standing seven feet high at the shoulder, weighing as much as 2,000 pounds. Since the days of Lewis and Clark, Indians had been killing the herds in large numbers, using the hides to make robes which were then traded for beads, whiskey, ammunition, and woolen clothing. By the mid-1840s, the Plains tribes were selling 100,000 hides each year to the American Fur Company and trading in similiar numbers at Bent's Fort and its satellite posts in eastern Colorado. The Indians also used large numbers of hides themselves for conical tipi covers and clothing. The brains, the sinew, the hoofs, and other parts of the buffalo's body had uses as well. But no matter how many head the Indians killed, the herds continued to thrive.

The truly brutal slaughter occurred between 1870 and 1883, when hunters swarmed the plains, shooting buffalo, skinning them, and leaving the carcasses to rot. As cheap rail transportation opened up the West, passengers often used passing herds for target practice, not even bothering to collect their trophies, but simply leaving the animals where they fell. A myth that killing a buffalo made a man more masculine contributed to the slaughter.

For a decade, more than a million buffalo were killed each year. The hides sold for up to three dollars each and the bones drew five dollars a ton. In 1874, the Santa Fe railroad alone hauled 3,500 tons of bones out of western Kansas and eastern Colorado. By 1883, the herds were virtually gone and the Indians were soon to follow.

By the 1890s decades of slaughter had left the American bison almost extinct.

most dramatic battles of the Indian Wars was still to come.

The origins of the dramatic affair can be traced to Oklahoma Territory where, in September 1878, a native leader named Dull Knife stole away from his exile there, taking with him 90 men, 120 women, and 141 children. This band fought its way across Kansas and parts of Nebraska before eluding its pursuers. But the toil of the trip proved to be too much for the children and the elderly, and Dull Knife sought to seek shelter at the Red Cloud Agency, unaware of its relocation. Upon his arrival in October at the old location, Dull Knife and his 149 Cheyenne were taken captive by the soldiers of Camp Robinson and confined to log barracks while they awaited the Indian Bureau's decision as to their fate. The answer came three months later—in January—when the Cheyenne were told they had to return to Oklahoma. Dull Knife refused to comply with the order. Consequently, his barracks were chained shut, and food and firewood were denied him and his band. After six days and nights, Dull Knife and his warriors reassembled guns they had hidden, attacked the sentries, and fled. The army took off in pursuit and the ensuing battle ended with 64 Cheyenne dead and 78 recaptured. Eleven soldiers perished and ten were wounded.

By the 1880s, Camp Robinson had become a fort, the army having decided that any permanent or long-term installation merited such a designation. During this decade, Fort Robinson's days were filled with routine target practice, inspections, and the construction of new buildings. The 23,000-acre military outpost expanded with adobe officers' quarters, as well as barracks, stables, and storehouses. Settlement of the region continued, and a town, Crawford, sprang up. Among those assigned to the outpost was an African-American unit, the Ninth Cavalry. Their presence created tension between the military and the townfolk, but the Ninth proved to be a gallant unit, whose members distinguished themselves in subsequent engagements with the Indians.

Fort Robinson has undergone a number of changes in the ensuing years. It has been home to the Army Olympic equestrian team, the Quarter-master's Remount Depot, and the K-9 Corps during World War II, when it also housed German prisoners of war. Today, it's the largest state park in Nebraska, with tours of the grounds available by horseback, stagecoach, or wagon train. Original and reconstructed buildings help tell the story of this outpost's exciting past.

(top) Red Cloud, chief of the Sioux, for whom the Indian agency at Fort Robinson was named.

(above) Dull Knife (right), who led a band of Cheyenne out of the Indian Territory in September 1878, was placed under house arrest at Fort Robinson after he and his party sought shelter at the Red Cloud Agency.

(left) The Fort Robinson museum was once the post headquarters. Today it houses an impressive collection of artifacts, literature, and interpretive displays.

DEC. 29 1890

CANKPE OPI EL TONK

WICAKTE HI CUN HE OZ?EST KTE

1 CHIEF BIG FOOT
2 MR. HIGH HAWK
3 MR. SHADING BEAR
4 LONG BULL
5 WHITE AMERICAN
6 BLACK COYATE
7 GHOST HORSE
8 LIVING BEAR
9 AFRAID OF BEAR
10 YOUNG AFRAID OF BEAR
11 YELLOW ROBE
12 WOUNDED HAND
13 RED EAGLE
14 PRETTY HAWK
15 WM. HORN CLOUD
16 SHERMAN HORN CLOUD
17 SCATTERS THEM
18 RED FISH
19 SWIFT BIRD
20 HE CROW
21 LITTLE WATER

(*above*) A cemetery marks the site near Wounded Knee Creek in South Dakota where, on December 29, 1890, at least 200 Indian men, women, and children were killed at the hands of the Seventh Cavalry.

(*opposite*) This monument in the Indian cemetery carries the names of 22 of the Sioux braves who were killed in the massacre. Among the names are the chief, Big Foot, and Mr. High Hawk, Ghost Horse, William and Sherman Horn Cloud, and He Crow.

The end of the 19th century saw most Native Americans stripped of their freedom and dignity and reduced to living on reservations. They were hungry, hard-hit by disease, and desperate. So they listened and believed when a Nevada Pauite named Wovoka, considered to be a prophet, told them that by performing a so-called Ghost Dance and other rituals they could guarantee the eradication of the white man and the return of both their lands and the buffalo.

The Ghost Dance was performed with such enthusiasm on the South Dakota Sioux reservations that the army became worried about possible unrest and moved in. Increasing tensions reached a climax on December 15, 1890, when Chief Sitting Bull, a supporter of the Ghost Dancers, was killed by reservation police while allegedly resisting arrest. In the wake of Sitting Bull's death, a few hundred Sioux fled the Standing Rock Reservation and headed for the Badlands, where they planned to hide. Because they had left their reservation, the Indians were classified as hostiles, and the army set out after them. On the night of December 28, the Sioux surrendered to units

Sitting Bull

Sitting Bull was born in 1831 at Grand River, in what is now South Dakota. He was the only son of a warrior called Returns-Again, who named the child "Slow" for his careful and deliberate ways. A mystic, Returns-Again changed his own name to Sitting Bull long before the name was adopted by his son—when he heard it whispered one night by a buffalo.

Slow was raised in the warrior tradition, hearing the stories of battle. Like all male Sioux youngsters, he was given a coup stick at age 14, a slender wand that would give him prestige if he touched the enemy with it during battle. His chance came shortly thereafter, in a raid to capture horses from the Crows. The teeneager performed admirably and was renamed Sitting Bull.

The young Sitting Bull was not physically attractive, but he still married nine times, a courteous and gentle man to his wives. By 25, he was a leader of the elite military society known as the Strong Hearts. His peers considered him headstrong and fearless.

Sitting Bull, inaugurated a Sioux Chief in the 1860s, spent his life fighting efforts by outsiders—notably whites—to reduce Sioux territory. An impassioned speaker, he denounced treaties with the U.S. government when they threatened his ancestral land.

In 1872, Sitting Bull committed an act for which he became famous. During an engagement between the

Sitting Bull in a photo taken in 1885.

army and the Sioux over unceded land, the chief strode into the center of the battle, sat down, and filled, lit, and smoked his pipe while bullets whizzed past him. He didn't move until the pipe was finished and cleaned.

Sitting Bull took part in many battles but none so famous as Custer's Last Stand at the Little Bighorn River in June 1876. This was his moment of greatest triumph. It also marked the beginning of the end for the Sioux. Sitting Bull fled to Canada in 1877 but, four years later, became homesick and returned to the United States and reservation life. For a time, he traveled as part of Buffalo Bill Cody's Wild West show. He was killed nine years later, at the age of 59, by an Indian reservation policeman.

of the Seventh Cavalry near Wounded Knee Creek in South Dakota. The soldiers surrounded the Indian camp but the two opposing parties managed to pass the night in relative peace, though both sides were nervous. The next day, however, the soldiers attempted to strip the Indians of their weapons. Suddenly, according to one account, a fight erupted over a young brave's new rifle. A shot rang out and, from within a mass of struggling men, a trooper fell.

The massacre that ensued was almost incomprehensible. The soldiers began firing at the Sioux at close range, slaughtering them where they sat. The Indians were virtually unable to retaliate. Most were unarmed. The few that possessed clubs or knives which they had hidden in their blankets found their weapons useless against the soldiers' arms. Indians who attempted to escape were hunted down, many of them killed miles from the camp. While about 25 soldiers died during the altercation, the final Indian death toll is uncertain because the Sioux later removed some of the bodies, making an accurate count impossible. Still, it is believed that at least 200 Indian men, women, and children were killed. Many of the dead, including 18 children and 44 women, were buried in a mass grave on January 2, when the weather allowed the army to return.

The Battle at Wounded Knee marked the virtual end of the military engagements between whites and Native Americans that had prevailed for more than two centuries. But it became the site of another battle a few generations later. On February 27, 1973, approximately 200 members of the American Indian Movement (AIM) took the reservation town of Wounded Knee by force. Declaring it the "Independent Oglala Sioux Nation," they announced that they would remain on the site until the U.S. government met their demands for a

(above) The draw at the massacre site. The Battle at Wounded Knee marked the virtual end of the military engagements between whites and Native Americans that had prevailed for more than two centuries.

(right) The Sioux leader, Big Foot, was found frozen in the snow in the aftermath of the Wounded Knee massacre.

change in tribal leaders, a review of all Indian treaties, and a Senate investigation of the treatment accorded Indians in general. Federal marshals were called in and a siege began, lasting until May 8, when the Indians surrendered in exchange for the promise of negotiations. During the standoff, two Indians were killed and one federal marshal seriously wounded. To this day, Wounded Knee remains a poignant national symbol of the injustices suffered by Native Americans.

FORT MEADE

STURGIS, SOUTH DAKOTA

(above) Legend has it that Gen. Philip Sheridan, the commander of army operations in the West, rode his horse about Fort Meade's future parade ground, seen here, grandly pointing his saber at the spot where he wanted each new building constructed.

(opposite) The guard house, constructed in 1900 of local sandstone, became a post office in 1945, when a Veterans Administration hospital acquired the site. It remains a post office today.

Fort Meade was established during the winter of 1878/79 to provide military protection for settlers and prospectors who had invaded the Dakota Territory after gold was discovered in the Black Hills. The indigenous Sioux were resentful of these newcomers, and hostile to them, both before and after the Black Hills Treaty of 1877, a treaty which was supposed to guarantee them certain land rights. Gold had a way of making men a little crazy—and the Sioux watched as their land was taken over by fortune-seekers, and their way of life destroyed.

Gen. Philip Sheridan, the famed Civil War cavalry leader, selected the fort's site. It is claimed that he rode about the future parade ground on horseback, grandly pointing his saber at the spot where he wanted each new building constructed on the 12-square-mile military reservation.

The new fort replaced Camp J. C. Sturgis, established in July 1878, about two miles northwest of the nearby Bear Butte. Fort Meade was originally named Camp Ruhlen, for Lt. George Ruhlen, the 17th Infantry quartermaster officer who supervised its construction. It was renamed to honor

(above) The post's first permanent commander, Col. Samuel D. Sturgis, resided in these imposing quarters. A Union general during the Civil War, Sturgis was one of the founders of the South Dakota town that bears his name.

(right) After gold was discovered in the Black Hills during the 1870s, prospectors and fortune-seekers invaded what was then Indian land. Seen here, in a photo from 1889, are "old timers" Spriggs, Lamb, and Dillon.

Gen. George Meade, the commanding general of the Union forces during the Civil War and the victor of the Battle of Gettysburg.

The ten-company post was strategically located at the mouth of a natural gap in the hogback ridge that formed the outer rim of the Black Hills. It was along the main Indian trail that led to the Sioux's favorite hunting ground. It was also near the confluence of the heavily traveled Bismarck, Fort Pierre, and Sidney trails, a setting that helped Fort Meade play an important role in maintaining peace on the western Dakota frontier.

The Seventh Cavalry, reformed after the terrible Battle of the Little Big Horn in 1876, was the post's first permanent garrison. The first permanent commander was Col. Samuel D. Sturgis, a Union general during the Civil War, and one of the founders of the nearby town that bears his name.

Fort Meade boasts association with a number of interesting historical events. It was here that the cavalry horse Comanche, the lone U.S. survivor of Custer's Last Stand, was retired with military honors. This was also the place where Maj. Marcus Reno, who had been with Custer just before the fatal battle of Little Big Horn, ended his military career. He was court-martialed here for "scandalous behavior." The Star-Spangled Banner first became the official music for the military retreat ceremony at Fort Meade, long before it became the national anthem. And a number of celebrated frontier army units saw service at Fort Meade,

Philip Sheridan

Philip Henry Sheridan was not exactly the picture of a dashing cavalry officer. The famed Civil War general was a small man with abnormally long arms, and he usually dressed in mismatched and rumpled clothes. His head was massive and misshapen, so oddly formed that he made most of his charges bareheaded. While his supporters attributed this to gallantry, the reality was that he simply couldn't keep a hat on.

Despite his appearance, Sheridan was popular with the ladies. He was a noted conversationalist, loved dancing, and enjoyed the theater. Although he relished the good life, the general was equally at home in the field, where he marched with his troops and endured their hardships.

Born to Irish immigrants in Albany, New York, in 1831, Sheridan graduated from West Point in 1853. After the Civil War, "Little Phil," as his men called him, served briefly as the military governor of Louisiana. He was then assigned command of army operations in the West.

If Sheridan was supportive of his men, he was brutal to his enemies. In 1868, for example, he began a destructive winter campaign against the Plains Indians, aimed at women and children as well as warriors. His objective was clear—to destroy all Indians. This obsession, which persisted throughout his career, was particularly directed toward the Sioux. Accordingly, one of his favorite officers was George Armstrong Custer, an expert at attacking Native American settlements. Sheridan came to admire the headstrong, impulsive man the Indians called "Yellow Hair."

In 1884, Sheridan became general-in-chief of the army upon the death of William Tecumseh Sherman. He died, while on leave, in Nonquitt, Massachusetts, in 1888.

Gen. Philip Sheridan at the time of the Civil War, wearing his favorite porkpie hat.

including the Fourth Cavalry, which was headquartered here for more than 20 years.

Fort Meade outlived all other frontier posts on the lands of the Upper Missouri, surviving as a military installation until 1944, when it became a Veterans Administration Hospital. Many remnants of the old post, located one mile east of Sturgis, South Dakota, have been faithfully preserved, and the Old Fort Meade Museum displays uniforms, weapons, and other mementos of the troopers who served here. One of the fort's more curious artifacts can be found in the Old Post Cemetery. It's a monument to "two of the heaviest drinkers in Troop D, Eighth Cavalry."

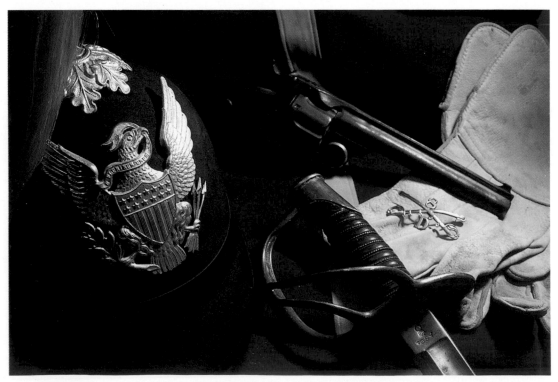

(opposite) Artifacts pertaining to Fort Meade's colorful history include a parade helmet with pompadour and gloves, all from 1880, and a spike dating from 1872 to 1888.

(above) Fort Meade was established during the winter of 1878/79 to provide protection for settlers and prospectors who had invaded the Dakota Territory after gold was discovered in the Black Hills.

(top right) Officers of the Eighth Cavalry at Fort Meade in 1892.

(right) During the fort's heyday, a stable, such as the one seen here, would have housed up to 86 horses. A harness repair shop would have been found on the premises as well.

(*above*) In 1864, under the direction of post commander Maj. Robert Rose, construction of Fort Sisseton took shape. In addition to oak blockhouses and a saw mill, there was also a commissary and quartermaster's storehouse, a hospital, stables, officers' quarters, and a cemetery.

(*opposite*) A stable was a pivotal building on any military outpost of the 19th century. The one at Fort Sisseton had 78 stalls.

In the years between 1806 and 1861, pioneers arrived in great numbers in what became the states of Minnesota and Iowa. They hunted buffalo, trapped furs, farmed, built settlements, and traded with the Native Americans. Treaties were established, which reserved certain lands for the indigenous people and for the payment of annuities to maintain the reservations. However, during the Civil War (1861–1865), the United States government neglected to maintain its obligations and the Indians nearly starved as crop failure along with tardy federal payments created a crisis situation. In 1862, the Indians rose up in protest, claiming the lives of 800 white men, women, and children across southern Minnesota, Dakota, and northern Iowa. This uprising forced the army to establish a permanent presence in the area. To that end, a series of border forts was planned. Among them was a post to be established in the Coteau des Prairies area known as Kettle Lakes, where there was abundant water, timber, fuel, and clay. A location was secured, and, even before any construction began in 1864, four cannon were mounted, one facing in each direction.

Initially the post was called Fort Wadsworth, but in 1876, when its occupants learned of a fort by that designa-

Capt. Clarence Bennett, who served at Sisseton from 1878 to 1883, promoted new construction at the fort, adding a schoolroom and library, a brick carpenter's shop, and a blacksmith's shop during his tenure.

Fort Sisseton's principal role was to protect settlers in the area from Indian attacks. Consequently, blockhouses like this one were the first buildings to be constructed on the post.

Indian Scouts

As the army battled its way across the West, it became obvious that one of the greatest advantages the Native Americans possessed was their intimate knowledge of the terrain. War parties could easily evade troops and select sites for engagements that would give them a strategic advantage.

The army had been using scouts—notably mountain men such as Jim Bridger and Kit Carson—to travel in advance of troops, looking for hostiles and helping to plan travel routes. But experienced hands soon realized they would fare even better if they could obtain the services of friendly Indians. Not only could native scouts provide a knowledge of the terrain and bring their tracking skills to bear, they could serve as interpreters and help to reassure friendly tribes resisting surrender for fear of mistreatment.

The Indian scouts quickly proved their worth, astonishing soldiers with their ability to determine the age of a trail by studying the discoloration of a grass patch or to determine the tribal branch to which fleeing warriors belonged by studying their moccasin prints. They were used throughout the West, and the army came to believe the proverb "Only an Apache can catch an Apache." Indeed, some Indians became scouts straight from the warpath, seeking to use the power of the United States to take revenge on their tribal enemies.

These Native Americans took part in many of the major conflicts during the Indian Wars. A notable example was Scout Mitch Bouyer, a half-breed, who tried in vain to convince Gen. George Armstong Custer that the Little Big Horn Valley held more Indians than his band of cavalry could handle. When Custer ignored him, Bouyer and his fellow scouts stayed with the troopers, electing to die with their leader.

Indian scouts at Surrendered Camp, six miles northeast of Fort Sisseton.

tion in New York State, the name was changed to Fort Sisseton in honor of a nearby tribe, the Sisseton-Wapheton Indians, who served as military scouts and occupied a series of camps that surrounded the fort. The fort's complement of troops consisted of four companies and a light artillery battery. In addition to their military duties, the enlisted men were employed as common laborers, woodcutters, quarrymen, and mechanics, while many of the officers doubled as engineers and foremen. In mid-1864, Maj. Robert Rose arrived to become post commander. He carried on with construction and began to secure the fort's boundary. Soon there were blockhouses made of hewn oak, an earthen embankment, and a saw mill. Construction also began on the commissary and quartermaster's storehouse, a hospital, stables, officers' quarters, and a cemetery. Major Rose's first winter was a difficult one. While construction was in progress, his most urgent task was to provide adequate shelter for the men and animals under his command. Food was sometimes in short supply and scurvy began to break out. Many officers and enlisted men supplemented their meager rations by hunting and fishing.

During the first two years of the fort's existence, the very act of building a military outpost took most of the soldiers' time. There was little opportunity for drilling, and discipline problems arose.

The frontier life was a hard one. The men had to chop wood for fire and ice to use as drinking water. They maintained acres of gardens, and put up hay for the livestock. In addition to their basic survival duties, they also patrolled the frontier borders, maintaining a show of force to discourage the Indians and encourage white settlement. Wary pioneers were glad to see the uniformed men on patrol, but even these hardened troopers could not combat the bitter winter weather. During the frigid months, snowfalls would stop expeditions completely. In 1866, five men were lost in a snowstorm and perished. Their bodies were not found until spring.

Still Fort Sisseton was fortunate in having a doctor on the post. His records provide a grim testament to the hazards of frontier life. In one year, nine bodies were interred in the post cemetery due to typhoid, four to tuberculosis, two each from fever, drowning, bronchitis, pneumonia, meningitis, and "gun wounds received while deserting." Several infants died before reaching three months of age. To provide medical facilities, a brick hospital was constructed fronting the parade ground. It was 60 feet by 32 feet and plastered so poorly that Assistant Surgeon B. Knickerbocker complained, "the roof, ill constructed, freely admits wind and snow."

Over the years, the fort changed commanders and continued to grow. Capt. Clarence Bennett added a schoolroom and library in 1880 and 1881. He also built a brick carpenter's shop and blacksmith's shop during his tenure. At around the same time, the post surgeon gave the fort a gentler look, planting roses and flowers around the hospital to enhance its appearance.

The final improvements were made in 1885 when a porch was added to the soldiers' barracks.

In its later years, Fort Sisseton became known as a choice assignment for officers. By then, there was little threat of Indian attack and the elite enjoyed such luxuries as champagne, white tablecloths, and military orchestras. In 1886, the army decided to abandon the fort; as the tribes in the area had been pacified, it had outlived its usefulness. The final orders to vacate it were signed on June 1, 1889.

In 1920, Col. W. C. Boyce, a wealthy Chicago newspaperman, leased the fort, turning its main buildings into a hunting lodge. After his death in 1928, a number of uses for the fort were considered. Finally, in 1932, it became a historic site under the direction of the Fort Sisseton Memorial Association. Buildings were repaired according to use, rather than historical accuracy. In 1935, the National Park Service took over the site and began a careful restoration. In 1959, the South Dakota Legislature designated Fort Sisseton a state park. Today, guided tours of the grounds and the Visitor Center museum enable tourists to imagine what it was like to man a rugged frontier outpost during the 19th century.

In the foreground of this photo is the fort's magazine. Directly behind it is the original guardhouse, a one-story brick building that could accommodate 20 men.

During the first two years of the fort's existence, the very act of building a military outpost took most of the soldiers' time. There was little opportunity for drilling, and discipline problems arose.

(*above*) Fort Totten's stately looking Officers' Row belies the problems of construction and maintenance that these structures presented. The lakeshore climate caused the wood to rot and the bricks required constant repainting.

(*opposite*) The ruins of the enlisted men's barracks at Fort Totten. Each room could house up to 15 men. There were three such rooms on each of two floors and there were four barracks in total. These dwellings were converted to dormitories when the fort became a school.

The construction of Fort Totten began on July 19, 1867, when military units under the command of Gen. Alfred A. Terry built the original log buildings some 800 yards north of the fort's eventual and present site. Local raw materials were used for the brick, mortar, and much of the lumber. Named for Brevet Gen. Joseph Gilbert Totten (1788–1864), late Chief Engineer of the U.S. Army, the fort was erected to enforce the treaty agreements between the federal government and the local Native American tribes and to protect the overland route between southern Minnesota and western Montana. Cavalry and infantry units carried out what amounted to police functions. They patrolled the International Boundary, attempted to control the liquor traffic, guarded overland transportation routes, and protected both the residents of the Fort Totten Reservation and the nearby settlers.

The boredom at this isolated post created a number of problems. Other than routine patrols, daily drills, and housekeeping, there was little for the soldiers to do. Men were frequently put to the mundane tasks of repainting bricks to prevent their deterioration and replacing wood

roofs and windows affected by dry rot due to the lakeshore climate. A high rate of alcoholism developed and desertions from the fort were frequent. There were few chances for military action and, when they did occur, results were often tragic. In the most notorious instance, units of the Seventh Cavalry were among those called to serve in the 1876 Sioux campaign that led to the death of Gen. George Custer and his troops at the Little Big Horn River.

Decommissioned in December 1890, the post became the property of the Bureau of Indian Affairs on January 5, 1891, and for the next 45 years it served as an Indian industrial school. The role of educational institution was fitting, for Fort Totten had inaugurated an education program for Indians as early as 1874. In those days, it was the Wapheton, Sisseton, and Cuthead bands of Sioux who lived near the fort. The Grey Nuns of Montreal had established the first school for these Native Americans.

Upon the fort's acquisition by the Bureau of Indian Affairs, many of its buildings were altered and a boarding school was opened. Students from reservations throughout the northern plains were removed from their families and provided with what was considered a practical education. Enrollment was high, sometimes exceeding 400. Girls were taught domestic skills, and given some business-related training, including typing, and boys were instructed in farming and industrial trades. The *(opposite)* The commanding officer's quarters, constructed of brick from local clay around 1840, included a parlor, a dining room, a library/office, a family sitting room, and four bedrooms. At the time, it was probably the finest mansion in the area.

(right) This display, drawn from the establishment of William Plummer & Son, reflects the kind of merchandise that was typically sold at a frontier general store around 1890. Mr. Plummer's store was located in the town of Minnewaukan, North Dakota.

The boredom at this isolated post created a number of problems. Other than routine patrols, daily drills, and housekeeping, there was little for the soldiers to do.

intent was to prepare Indian youths for life off of the reservation. As a result, these children were forced to abandon their native language and traditions. A changing federal policy toward Indian education brought about the closure of the school in 1935.

Fort Totten had its next incarnation as a tuberculosis preventorium for Native Americans. Between 1935 and 1939, patients came from reservations throughout the northern United States. If they were healthy enough, they received academic courses along with medical treatment.

In 1940, Fort Totten again became an educational institution, this time serving as an elementary school and high school for the surrounding community and those who boarded there. The staff, provided by the Bureau of Indian Affairs, mixed manual training with academic studies. The school's athletic teams were greatly respected in the Devil's Lake region and many students went on to become community leaders. But a new facility was constructed nearby and, in 1959, the Fort Totten Community School closed its doors.

Finally in 1960—almost 100 years after its construction—Fort Totten was transferred to the State Historical Society of North Dakota for use as a state historic site. Twelve miles south of Devil's Lake, it encompasses almost ten acres, and includes 16 of the 39 buildings that made up the fort. It is considered one of the best-preserved frontier military posts in the Trans-Mississippi area. Recent restoration efforts have included the development of an Interpretive Center, the Commanding Officer's quarters, the Pioneer Daughters' Museum, and the Fort Totten Little Theater.

(opposite) **At the ready with his breechload rifle is this "guard," attired in the uniform of an infantry officer circa 1890. Up to 400 men had been stationed at the post during its heyday in the 1870s, but upon occasion the number had dropped to 45 or less.**

Indian Schools

During the 18th and 19th centuries, white Americans believed their civilization to be inherently superior to that of the Indians. Consequently, as soon as an area was secured from the threat of hostile Indian attacks, well-meaning groups and individuals would attempt to "civilize" the local tribes. To this end, schools were often established specifically for Indian children.

The problems with attempting to educate a people with a completely different way of life and a distinctive set of beliefs were huge, and drastic measures seemed warranted. The children were forcibly removed from their families, taken from the only life they had ever known, and compelled to wear the white man's clothes, speak the white man's language, eat the white man's food, and play the white man's games. At the Carlisle Indian School in Pennsylvania, young Apache arrivals were even given new Anglo-Saxon names. The founder's motto was "Kill the Indian and save the man." Once the children learned enough English to get by, they were forbidden to speak their mother tongues.

No doubt there were intrinsic benefits to the training the Indian children received in these schools. Among other things, they learned to read and write English. But this system of education produced graduates who belonged to no one. They were indisputably Native Americans and not welcome in white society. On the other hand, they had been stripped of all ties to their families and were unable to even communicate with relatives. Some graduates did achieve a level of success, however. Athlete Jim Thorpe was enrolled at Carlisle in 1904 and went on to fame in the Olympics, in baseball, and football. Sadly, though, he was an exception.

The Fort Totten Indian School band gathered for this photo in 1908.

FORT UNION

WILLISTON, NORTH DAKOTA

(above) The bourgeois house at Fort Union stood at the north end of the post. Constructed in 1851, it was the most impressive structure at the fort, serving as both home and office to the company manager.

(opposite) The rough-and-ready trappers and mountain men lived simply, often adopting Indian customs as well as the Native American's nomadic lifestyle.

Kenneth McKenzie was a ruthless man. An employee of John Jacob Astor's American Fur Company, he set himself impossible goals—and usually achieved them. In 1829, the task that lay before him was the establishment of a company fort at the junction of the Missouri and Yellowstone rivers in what is now North Dakota. The post, which was called Fort Union, soon became a very busy place indeed, as McKenzie and the bold men that he hired traded beaver furs and buffalo robes with the Assiniboin Indians to the north and the Crow Indians to the southwest. Most surprisingly, McKenzie established trade relations with the Blackfeet who lived farther up the Missouri. The resolute Scotsman became known as the "King of the Missouri" and played the role to the hilt, drinking fine wines, wearing ruffled shirts, playing a bagpipe, and importing delicate furniture upriver by company steamboats.

The fort McKenzie built stood on a grassy plain that stretched north for a mile, providing ample room for Indian camps at trading time. The post was enclosed by a palisade of vertical logs, 220 feet by 240 feet. Employees occupied rooms in a long building on the west side while a matching

structure on the east side was home to a retail store and a warehouse for trade goods. The north end featured the imposing bourgeois house, Fort Union's most distinctive building and the post's administrative center. As the fort's first superintendent (or bourgeois), this was McKenzie's headquarters. Behind it stood a bell tower and a kitchen. The main gate opened on the south—or river—side; a second smaller gate led to the prairie lands. The fort also held a reception room for the Indians, shops for a blacksmith and tinsmith, an ice-house, a powder magazine, and enclosures for animals. Two-story stone bastions at the northeast and southwest corners of the fort served as observation posts and defensive positions.

In its heyday, Fort Union employed up to 100 men, many of whom were married to Indian women and had fam-

(left) **Hunters supplied the post with fresh meat—including buffalo, elk, or deer. A hunter's annual salary was $400. He received an additional fee for the hide and horns of each animal that he killed.**

(below) **Distributing goods to the Assinniboin Indians at Fort Union, in an unknown artist's rendition. The fort stood on a grassy plain that stretched north for a mile, providing ample room for Indian camps at trading time.**

ilies. There was an almost cosmopolitan flavor about the place, with Americans sharing quarters with English, German, French, Russian, Italian, and Spanish residents, and their families. The American Fur Company had a policy of helping travelers to visit its posts on the Missouri. Thus, adventurers, scientists, artists, and priests all came to Fort Union. John James Audubon was a guest, as was Prince Maximilian of Wied and his artist-companion Karl Bodmer.

For three decades, beaver was in great demand for hats. By the 1830s, however, silk top hats became the headware of fashion and beaver fell from demand. Fort Union, meanwhile, turned its focus to tanned buffalo robes as the trade item of choice. The abundance of bison on the plains, coupled with improved river transportation, enabled the outpost to make the transition from beaver to bison pelts with ease. Trading was brisk and successful, even in 1837, when smallpox swept McKenzie's domain. Thousands of Indians were killed. Especially hard hit were the Mandans, where estimates claim only 31 survived from a community of 1,600 people.

By the time of the Civil War's out-

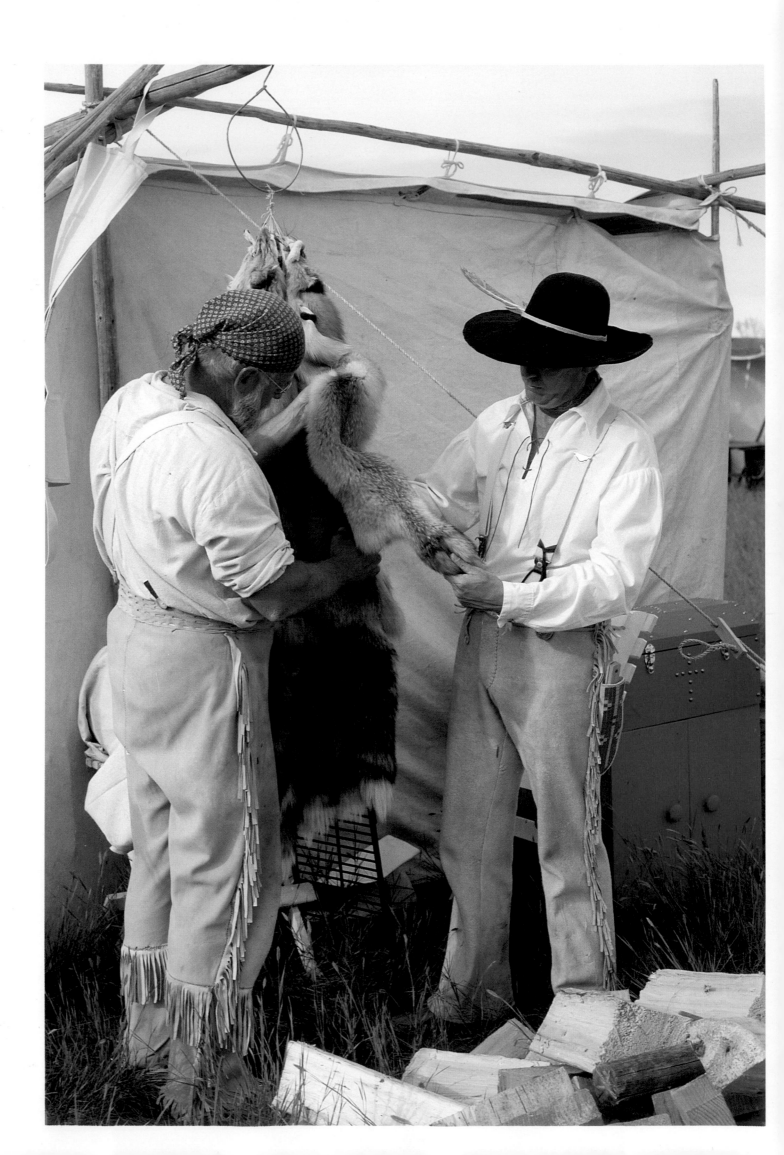

Prince Maximilian and Karl Bodmer

Not everyone traveling through the old West was a pioneer settler. There were also many naturalists and explorers, intent on discovering the flora and fauna of this wilderness.

One of the most distinguished adventurers was Prince Alexander Philip Maximilian of the German principality of Wied-Neuwied. Although he was royalty, Maximilian had not spent his life being coddled. Among other things, he served as a major general in the allied army during the Napoleonic Wars, leading a division in the 1814 capture of Paris.

Following the war, the prince spent two years exploring South America, and another ten writing two huge works on Brazil's natural environment. He also composed a detailed atlas of the country. The monarch then turned his eye to the American West, and sailed for the United States in 1832. He brought along the Swiss artist Karl Bodmer, to make a pictorial record of the royal expedition.

Bodmer produced 400 watercolor sketches of remarkable clarity and beauty as the pair traveled up the Missouri River in 1833. Although the prince dismissed Bodmer as merely "an able draughtsman," he would eventually find himself best known as the artist's sponsor. Bodmer's work was collected in a two-volume set of books called *Travels in the Interior of North America in the Years 1832–1834*. This work, considered to be the definitive European reference work on the American wilderness, was produced by the prince.

The Swiss artist Karl Bodmer produced a body of some 400 watercolors during his journey up the Missouri River with Prince Maximilian in 1833.

(opposite) An animal skin is examined thoroughly and the bargaining begins.

break in 1861, Fort Union had weathered another smallpox epidemic, Sioux hostilities, and the scattering of many Indian tribes, all of which led to a significant decline in trade. In the summer of 1864, the fort was described by one army general as "an old dilapidated affair, almost falling to pieces." In 1866, an infantry company arrived on the Upper Missouri and began constructing an army post nearby. Meanwhile, Fort Union was sold to the Northwest Fur Company, which tried to continue the post's trading activities but finally abandoned the effort. In 1867, the army acquired the post, which it dismantled, using the materials to complete the new fort.

Fort Union Trading Post National Historic Site is located 24 miles southwest of Williston, North Dakota, and 21 miles north of Sidney, Montana. Portions of the fort have been reconstructed, including the walls, stone bastions, Indian trade house, and the ornate bourgeois house, which is now the park's Visitors Center.

Initially, the fort that Kenneth McKenzie built in 1829 was enclosed by a palisade of vertical logs, 220 feet by 240 feet. It was built by hardy men with tools like the ax seen here.

(right) This skull serves as a silent reminder of the toll exacted on wildlife by American trappers, traders, and adventurers during the 19th century. A number of species—notably the bison—faced extinction or near extinction as a result of the wholesale slaughter of their numbers.

(far right) Kenneth McKenzie, an employee of John Jacob Astor's American Fur Company, established Fort Union in 1829.

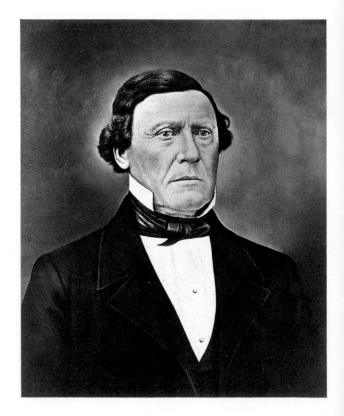

(*opposite*) A "trapper" at Fort Union's annual mountain man rendezvous demonstrates a fundamental skill in the art of wilderness survival.

(*below*) Mountain men carried few foodstuffs with them. For the most part, they lived off of the land, eating what they could kill or catch.

(above) Situated at the crossroads of the major overland trails, Bent's Old Fort became a principal stopping point for settlers, mountain men, traders, and Indians.

(opposite) Bent's Old Fort features adobe walls that are 15 feet high and 2 feet thick. The round-corner bastion in the distance housed cannon in the 1840s.

A trio of traders from St. Louis were responsible for the 1833/34 construction of the massive Bent's Fort on the Arkansas River in southeastern Colorado. This adobe structure was to become the most important depot and point of call between Independence, Missouri, and Santa Fe, New Mexico, a frontier hub from which American trade and influence radiated.

The three traders were brothers Charles and William Bent and their partner Ceran St. Vrain. All three men had had experience in the Upper Missouri fur trade and, armed with some capital and an entrepreneurial spirit, they set out for the Arkansas Valley in the late 1820s. Within a few years, Bent, St. Vrain & Company had become a very successful business. Its owners depended upon friendly relations with both Native Americans and Mexicans and upon the suppression of competition for their success. Their dealings with the southern Cheyenne, on whose ground the Old Fort stood, were friendly and fair. William Bent opposed the use of whiskey as barter, since alcoholic spirits had elsewhere produced devastating effects on tribes without prior exposure to such beverages. To further strengthen

The Santa Fe Trail

The Santa Fe Trail came into being, like many other developments in the West, due to the efforts of a quick-thinking and brave man—who saw the chance to make a great deal of money.

In 1821, the Mexicans declared their independence from Spain. An American entrepreneur named William Becknell chanced to be in the region, planning to trade with the local Indians. Upon hearing the news, he raced to Santa Fe, New Mexico, sold his goods, and rushed home to Missouri. Four months later, he was on the trail again, this time accompanied by three wagons groaning with luxuries to sell to the Mexicans.

The rugged Raton Pass in the Rocky Mountains was a passageway suitable only for pack mules. To get his wagons through, Beck

nell was forced to turn southwest, heading toward the Cimarron River and into an unknown region of rock and sand. The ground was level but so dry that members of the expedition were forced to slash their mule's ears and drink the blood to quench their thirst. The caravan made it safely, however, and Becknell earned a 2,000 percent profit from the sale of his goods.

Despite Becknell's discovery of the Cimarron Cutoff, which eliminated 100 miles from the old route, the journey from Missouri to Santa Fe remained a difficult one. It often took more than a month and there was a constant danger en route of Comanche attacks, as well as the persistent problems of hunger and thirst. Nonetheless, other wagon trains followed in Becknell's path, better prepared for the desert terrain and thus he became known as the "Father of the Sante Fe Trail."

A sketch of the Sante Fe Trail drawn by Lt. W. H. Emory, a member of Gen. Stephen W. Kearney's expedition to New Mexico in 1846.

Charles Bent, a principal of the trading firm of Bent, St. Vrain & Company, became the first governor of the Territory of New Mexico. He was killed by Indians in Taos.

his company's ties with the Cheyenne, William Bent married Owl Woman, daughter of Grey Thunder, a powerful tribal priest.

The trading activities at Bent's Old Fort were broken into three areas. First, goods manufactured in the East were imported by Bent, St. Vrain & Company along the Santa Fe Trail from Missouri. A portion of these goods were left at the fort, and the remainder traveled down the trail into Mexican territory where they were sold. Second, goods of Mexican or Navajo origin arrived at the fort on the return trips for sale there or transport to Missouri. The third source of commerce came from the local tribes who traded their buffalo robes for manufactured goods at the fort.

For 17 years, the Bents and St. Vrain ran a highly successful operation. They commanded immense power, rewriting prairie law, and influencing Indians and Mexicans alike. But they were finally undone by events far beyond their control. Relations between the United States and Mexico had long been strained and, with the approach

(right) The barracks room, built in 1833, was a residence for laborers working at the post. It was also used as an infirmary for travelers.

(below) The trade room was the nerve center of the fort, offering such items as candles, crackers, and other luxuries in exchange for buffalo robes and beaver pelts.

(above) Used by traders, trappers, hunters, and post employees, the dining room was the largest room in the fort. Although its fare was simple, it nonetheless provided a welcome respite for road-weary travelers.

(below) Charles' brother William Bent married the daughter of a powerful Cheyenne priest, thereby strengthening the company's ties with the Cheyenne.

of armed conflict between the two nations in 1846, the federal government designated the trading post as an advance base for the invasion of New Mexico. During the ensuing years, soldiers occupied the fort, government cattle overgrazed the pastures, and military stores piled up.

Along with the soldiers came hordes of gold seekers, settlers, and adventurers. They destroyed water sources, carelessly used up precious wood, and frightened away the bison. Tensions with the Indians rose and the days of rich trading potential with the region's tribes ended. Then Charles Bent was killed in a revolt in Taos. Thereafter, business plummeted, and St. Vrain left for New Mexico. In 1849, things got even worse as cholera swept through the tribes. Finally, the last of the three partners, William Bent, loaded his wagons, packed up his family and employees, and left his outpost forever.

Today the fort has been reconstructed to accurately reflect the hal-cyon days between 1845/46. Bent's Old Fort National Historic Site is eight miles east of La Junta, Colorado, and fifteen miles west of Las Animas on highway 194. Visitors to the site are invited to see more than 30 rooms, among them William Bent's quarters—his office, complete with fireplace, and his bedroom, featuring beds made of pallets of straw covered with Spanish blankets. Visitors can also view the quarters used in 1846 by Susan Magoffin, a 19-year-old woman who stopped at the fort with her husband en route to Santa Fe. Tragically, while in residence, she lost the baby she was carrying. During her ten-day stay, she kept a detailed diary which still stands as one of the most complete descriptions of the fort during its final days of glory. Her room had a dirt floor and featured two windows, an unusual luxury.

(opposite) Bent's Old Fort has been reconstructed to accurately reflect the halcyon days between 1845/46, when trappers like the fellow pictured here made the fort a bustling place.

The Northwest

FORT LARAMIE, WYOMING

(above) The parade ground at Fort Laramie with the long, two-story enlisted men's barracks in the distance.

(opposite) The post headquarters has been restored to resemble its appearance in the early 1860s. The fort's commander and his wife lived on the second floor.

(previous pages) The entrance to the reconstructed Fort Hall in Pocatello, Idaho.

ort Laramie, an outpost in the Wyoming wilderness, played a crucial role in the settlement of the American frontier. For more than 50 years, it was a landmark and a way station for the countless trappers, traders, missionaries, emigrants, Pony Express riders, and miners who made their way West.

In 1834, fur trader William Sublette was searching for a site for a trading post when he happened upon "Laramie's Point" on the Laramie River near its confluence with the Platte. Erecting Fort William on the site, he sent out runners to inform the neighboring Sioux and Cheyenne chiefs of his interest in trading for their buffalo robes. Sublette and partner Robert Campbell were moderately successful but it wasn't until the American Fur Company bought the post in 1836 that it became a major fur trade center. The AFC enjoyed a pleasant monopoly in the area until 1841, when a new trading post, Fort Platte, was built by a rival company a mile away. This incursion inspired the older established firm to replace its rotting wooden outpost with a larger adobe structure, which it named Fort John. But it became commonly known as Fort Laramie.

In the 1840s, as the fort's traders carried on a dwindling fur trade with the Indians, the post became a popular

The founder of Fort Laramie, William Sublette, had moderate success trading with the neighboring Sioux and Cheyenne chiefs but it wasn't until the American Fur Company bought the post in 1836 that it became a major fur trade center.

The barracks, located off of the parade ground, was the largest building at Fort Laramie. Soldiers slept in two large, open squad bays on the second floor.

Pony Express

In every era, people have wanted to communicate with friends, loved ones, and business partners from whom they were apart. For a brief but memorable time during the settlement of the West, the riders of the Pony Express were entrusted with the job of getting those missives through.

The service was created by Russell, Majors, and Waddell, a partnership that operated a giant freight and mail service between St. Joseph, Missouri, and Sacramento, California. The partners wanted to reduce the period of time—a gruelling eight weeks—that it took wagon trains to transport mail between the company's two terminuses. Thus, in April 1860, an overland mail express route was established and the Pony Express was born. Totaling a distance of 1,966 miles, the route stretched over mountains, plains, and deserts. Because the horses were to gallop all the way, the riders had to change mounts every 12 to 15 miles. To this end, a series of 119 relay stations were built. Five

hundred ponies were purchased, and 75 made the first run. Each expressman traveled 45 to 75 miles before turning the route over to a fresh rider. It was a bold, daring, and dangerous scheme but it worked. The Pony Express completed its run from Missouri to California in a mere 11 days, reducing by some six-and-a half weeks the previous delivery time. In 1861, Wells Fargo took over the western end of the route and printed postage stamps to use over the entire line.

Most of the riders were young boys under 18. Because they risked death daily at the hands of the Indians and the elements, orphans were preferred. And because every ounce of weight was precious, they tended to be short and wiry. Among these courageous and resourceful riders was Will Cody, hired when he was 14. He was later to become famous as Buffalo Bill Cody, star attraction of his own Wild West show.

The completion of the transcontinental telegraph in October 1861 ended the need for the Pony Express. While the service lasted a relatively brief period—only 19 months—it left its mark, becoming a legendary part of the vibrant history of the American West.

Most of the Pony Express riders were under 18 and, because every ounce of weight was precious, they tended to be short and wiry.

stopping point for the large wagon trains following the Oregon Trail. The fort's strategic location on the 2,000-mile route that carried thousands of people from western Missouri to the Pacific Northwest gave the owners of Fort Laramie a bustling business in the sale of supplies to travelers.

The early years of immigration saw friendly relations between the Indians and whites, but as the flood of settlers increased, young warriors began to harass wagon trains. Consequently, in 1849, the army decided to increase its presence in the area, acquiring Fort

Laramie as a military installation. While the old fort was still in use, the army also began work on a new post laid out around a large parade ground. Although the soldiers assigned to Fort Laramie were there to protect the pioneers, actual combat between the garrison and neighboring tribes was rare. Most soldiers never saw a hostile Indian. Instead, the men settled into a routine of drills and mundane duties, relieved by the occasional foray off of the post to acquire liquor. The life was harsh, particularly for the recent arrivals from Europe who made up a large part of the frontier army. The

desertion rate in the army between 1865 and 1890 averaged 33 percent.

The fort was only attacked once. In summer 1864, a small cavalry unit back from patrol had just unsaddled its horses when a group of about 30 mounted warriors swept in, rounded up the mounts, and made their escape. The soldiers attempted a chase, but the Indians eluded them.

As the conflicts with Native Americans escalated in the 1850s and 1860s, the fort grew in importance. Its role was particularly enhanced as the Oregon Trail became the nation's major

overland mail route, the Civil War having eliminated the southern passageway. Even if the southern route had been open, the Pony Express, using Fort Laramie as a major way station, proved the superiority of the northern passageway.

As the flow of emigrants slowed in the 1860s, the fort became largely a staging ground for campaigns against the Indians, although it did continue to serve as a buffer between whites and the few defiant Native Americans in the area. In 1890, the year of the Battle of Wounded Knee, which effectively ended the Indian Wars, Fort Laramie was abandoned, its buildings sold at public auction.

The present historic site is about three miles southwest of the town of Fort Laramie, Wyoming. Many of the fort's important structures have sur-

Most of the soldiers stationed at Fort Laramie never saw a hostile Indian. Instead, the men settled into a routine of drills and mundane duties.

The lime-concrete post surgeon's quarters, built in 1875, are furnished in the Victorian style with ornate chairs, window coverings, and even a piano. The front parlor is seen here.

vived intact and nearly a dozen have been completely restored to their original appearance. One of the most significant restorations at the post is "Old Bedlam," the former bachelor officers' quarters and post headquarters.

(above) The schoolhouse at Fort Bridger (right) was built in 1860, the first such institution in the state of Wyoming. Appropriately, the milkhouse was next door.

(opposite) Jim Bridger's crudely fashioned trading post played a number of roles over the years. In addition to serving as a supply station and rest stop for pioneers heading West, it also became a Pony Express station, a military post, and the agency for the Shoshone Indians.

Few outposts in the West encapsulate as much frontier history as Fort Bridger, which originally served as a trading post for pioneers on the Oregon Trail, a way station for the Pony Express and the Overland Stage, and a military outpost during the Indian Wars.

The post was founded in 1843 by Jim Bridger and his partner, Louis Vasquez, to serve as a blacksmith shop and supply depot for Easterners making the trek to the Oregon Territory. The place they chose near Black's Fork on the Green River in what is now southwestern Wyoming was a natural stopping point for these travelers, the ideal spot for an outpost. The original Fort Bridger was ramshackle, consisting of several rough log buildings and a corral enclosed by a log stockade.

Jim Bridger was a true pioneer. He was born in Richmond, Virginia, in 1804, and moved to St. Louis, Missouri, in his childhood. In 1822, when he was just 18, he went West as a member of the Ashley-Henry Fur Company and quickly established a reputation as a trapper, hunter, and guide during the height of the beaver-trade era. In time, fashions changed and the demand for beaver pelts diminished, but by then the number of emigrants trekking through Bridger's area had given him a new line of work.

Among the varied lot of these emigrants who traversed through the region were the Mormons fleeing persecution in the East. Their leader, Brigham Young, and other church elders decided that they needed a depot where their followers could rest and obtain needed supplies on their journey to the Mormon State of Deseret—later the Territory of Utah—established in 1847. In 1853, the Mormons built Fort Supply approximately 12 miles south of Fort Bridger. Two years later, the religious group bought the Bridger-Vasquez post from Vasquez and used both forts to provision members of their faith and other emigrants.

The Mormon occupation lasted only two years, as friction rapidly developed between the newly established Mormon state and the United States government. In 1857, President James Buchanan dispatched troops to the area. When the Mormons spotted an advance army led by Col. Albert Sidney Johnston (and guided by Jim Bridger) they burned the forts and fled to their capital, Salt Lake City. When the army arrived at Fort Bridger, it

found only charred remains. Johnston ordered the establishment of a temporary camp, known as Camp Scott, close to the original site, where his troops remained for the winter. In spring 1858, Johnston continued on to Salt Lake City with the main body of his force, leaving some men behind with orders to rebuild a permanent fort. They did, utilizing a cobblestone wall left as a legacy of the Mormons. By 1859, 29 buildings had been constructed.

During the 1860s, the fort served as a way station for the Pony Express and the Overland Stage. Then came the Civil War and Fort Bridger's military personnel were ordered East. The fort was without troops for almost a year until W. A. Carter, post sutler organized a volunteer militia of local citizens. Other volunteer regiments—from Nevada and California—garrisoned there from 1862 to 1866. Thereafter, regulars again occupied the fort, this time in the form of two infantry companies under Brevet Maj. Andrew S. Burt. At one point, as many as 350 infantrymen were garrisoned at Bridger.

By the late 1860s, the fort played a variety of roles. Its soldiers escorted work crews from the Union Pacific as they made their way West toward

The commanding officer's quarters, built in 1884, brought a touch of refinement to the rugged outpost. It featured large area rugs, finely turned chairs, and even a stereoptican slide viewer.

When guards were off duty, they could relax here in the guards' room. The open door in the left rear of the photo leads to the general confinement cell. There were several solitary confinement cells as well.

Jim Bridger

Jim Bridger was born in Virginia in 1804 and came to St. Louis as a boy. By the time he was 18, during the height of the beaver trapping era, he was established as a trapper, hunter, and guide. According to the man himself, he discovered the Great Salt Lake in 1825. As he told it, he had started from the Wyoming border, followed the Bear River to its end and discovered a bay whose waters tasted salty. At the time, he thought that he had found an arm of the Pacific Ocean.

Bridger's physical courage became the stuff of legend. It is claimed, for example, that he spent three years with a long, barbed Blackfoot arrowhead buried deep in the muscles of his back and, when it was finally removed by a missionary/physician, he had only a bottle of whiskey to dull the pain.

During his early years, Bridger traveled with Jim Baker, another famous mountain man who later became an army scout and then guide to emigrant trains. By 1843, Bridger had established the fort that bore his name, a trading post for pioneers on their way West. After the fur trade had died out and Bridger had sold his fort, he returned to his home state of Missouri and became a farmer. He died peacefully in 1881.

Bridger had been one of the last of his kind. A mountain man, an explorer, and a guide, he helped to map the West. Of his own life and adventures, he once remarked: "They said I was the damndest liar ever lived. That's what a man gets for telling the truth."

Trapper, hunter, and guide, Jim Bridger claimed to have discovered the Great Salt Lake in 1825.

completion of the first transcontinental railroad. It served as a supply center for troops in the western portion of the Wyoming Territory. It helped provision geological, paleontological, and mining expeditions active in the area in the 1870s. And it served as the agency for the Shoshone Indians.

When peace finally came to the valley, the post was abandoned in 1878, but it was reactivated two years later, following an uprising of Ute Indians in Colorado. Additional barracks and quarters were built and general improvements made. In 1884, further construction took place with stone structures added, a water line laid, and the post commander's house built. Finally, on November 6, 1890, the last detachment of soldiers left, this time for good. The fort became a community center and the private home of Judge W. A. Carter. Many of the fort buildings were sold at auction and moved to other locations. Some can be seen, remodelled, in the Fort Bridger area. In the late 1920s, the State of Wyoming acquired the site. Since then, Fort Bridger has been preserved and maintained as a lasting reminder of Wyoming's colorful past.

The commanding officer's quarters reflect the typical design of military buildings during the 1880s. But with ten rooms, it was larger than the norm. The first commander had had extra bedrooms built so that his friends could visit him and enjoy the area's hunting and fishing.

(opposite) In 1857, Col. Albert Sidney Johnston led the federal troops against the Mormons in what became known as the Utah War. Johnston later distinguished himself with the Confederacy during the Civil War.

(opposite) The new guardhouse was erected in 1887 after a prisoner escaped from the old facility, another stone structure, by loosening the mortar in his cell's exterior wall. The new guardhouse had interior cells to prevent such jailbreaks.

(right) Troopers pose for an undated photograph in front of the commissary at Fort Bridger.

(below) The original Fort Bridger, founded in 1843, was ramshackle, consisting of several rough log buildings and a corral enclosed by a log stockade. In the 1880s, stone structures were added and a water line laid.

SOLDIERS.
JAMES QUINN.
WM. REED.
D. L. SYMMS.
J. E. TROY.
W. B. WHALEY.
R. H. HUGHES.
E. F. CLEAR.
WM. CASHAN.
A. B. WARREN.
JNO. SEILER.
W. H. HEATH.
C. E. ADAMS.
JNO. BURKE.
WM. DYE.
JNO. DUGGAN.
J. J. GALVAN.
LOUIS HAUGGI.
JNO. MILLER.
PETER McCUE.
W. B. ROGERS.
CHAS. SCHMIDT.
CHAS. SCOTT.
AND'W SNOW.
E. D. TESSIER.
T. S. TWEED.
M. F. O'HARA.
H. M. SCOLLIN.
FRED'K STREING.
HENRY GORDON.
GEO. LORENTZ.
W. D. MEYER.
C. E. SMITH.
J. J. TAUNER.
HENRY TURLEY.
F. F. HUGHES.
H. C. VOIGT.
ANTHONY ASSADILY.
T. E. MAXWELL.
WM. ANDREWS.
ELMER BABCOCK.
AMI CHEEVER.
W. B. CRISFIELD.
CHAS. GRAHAM.
WESTON HARRINGTON.
HENRY HAMILTON.
T. G. KAVANAGH.
LOUIS LOBERING.
CHAS. McCARTHY.
D. J. O'CONNELL.
CHRISTIAN REIBOLD
HENRY ROBERTS.
BENT SIEMONSON.
BYRON TARBOX.
MICH'L VETTER.
HENRY KLOTZBUCHER.
DAVID SUMMERS.
BARTHOLOMEW MAHONEY.
ARIKAREE INDIAN SCOUTS.
BLOODY KNIFE.
BOBTAILED BULL.
LITTLE SOLDIER.
CIVILIANS.
BOSTON CUSTER.
MARK KELLOGG.
ARTHUR REED.
CHAS. REYNOLDS.
MITCH BOYER.
F. C. MANN.
ISAIAH.

(above) The headstone with the black shield commemorates the original grave of George Armstrong Custer. His remains were later reburied on the grounds of West Point, from which Custer had graduated.

(opposite) A monument marks the place where Custer made his "last stand." It bears the names of all the dead soldiers.

Even those with only a passing knowledge of the history of the United States are familiar with the Battle of the Little Big Horn. It stands as a symbol of an evolving nation—a symbol that incorporates both heroism and tragedy, bravery and humiliation, victory and the very worst of defeats. It is inextricably linked with one of the most enigmatic and controversial military figures in U.S. history, George Armstrong Custer.

The Battle of the Little Big Horn was merely one skirmish in a centuries-old conflict that began when Europeans first set foot in North America. The newcomers and the Native Americans had clashed almost from the start. The result was a litany of destruction, death, despair, and misunderstanding. The conflict reached its pinnacle following the Civil War, as hoards of settlers streamed across the Great Plains. These emigrants were, for the most part, ignorant of the customs and culture of the Indians. They showed little regard for the sanctity of hunting grounds or the terms of former treaties.

In 1868, the U.S. government signed a treaty at Fort Laramie, reserving all of the land in present-day western South Dakota exclusively for the Sioux. In addition, por-

George Armstrong Custer

At the tender age of 23, George Armstrong Custer became a general. He went directly from the grade of lieutenant to that exalted rank because he so impressed his commander, Gen. Alfred Pleasanton, at the Battle of Aldie, Virginia, during the Civil War that Pleasanton promoted him on the spot. But the "Boy General," as they called him, was never really a true soldier in the hard-bitten military sense; rather, he was somewhat soft, preferring musicales, amateur theatrics, and riding to more warlike endeavors.

Born the son of an Ohio blacksmith in 1839, Custer entered West Point in 1857, graduating last in his class of 34. In 1864, he married Elizabeth Bacon, considered to be the prettiest girl in New Rumley, Ohio, the small town where they both spent their childhoods. The pair were devoted, and Libbie was constantly with her husband, except when he was on campaign. Although he loved his wife, Custer took a somewhat relaxed view toward his marriage vows, engaging in affairs with other women from time to time.

The Custers never had children. George's love went to his pets, which ran the gamut from a mouse to a wolf. His pack of dogs grew to 40, all of them spoiled by the general. Wrote Libbie of the canines,

"If I secured a place in the bed, I was fortunate."

In the opinion of many, Custer was brave, but not especially skilled in the art of war. He was poor at tactical moves and often attacked without reconnoitering. Moreover, his men disliked him, feeling that he cared little for their welfare. But perhaps Custer's greatest failing was his ego. Those who knew him believed that he was interested in running for president of the United States and, in that regard, was in a hurry to build a name for himself as an Indian fighter. He saw the 1876 campaign against the Sioux as a major opportunity to enhance his reputation. But his rashness as a commander had caught up with him, and, instead of glory at the Little Big Horn, he found death. He was 37.

George Armstrong Custer in a photo taken on about April 23, 1876, two months and two days before the Battle of the Little Big Horn.

tions of southeastern Montana and northeastern Wyoming were set aside as unceded territory to be used by the tribe for hunting. Peace lasted until 1874, when gold was discovered in the Black Hills in the heart of the Indian territory, and thousands of gold seekers swarmed the region in violation of the Fort Laramie treaty. Hostilities erupted as whites encroached upon Indian territory, and escalated to the point where Native Americans were leaving the reservation and attacking settlements and travelers on lands beyond their domain. To put a stop to the raids, the government tried to purchase the Black Hills but the Sioux, who considered the mountains sacred, refused to sell. Then, in December 1875, the government ordered the tribes to return to their own territory. When they did not comply, the army was called in to enforce the order.

The campaign of 1876 consisted of three separate expeditions, one under Gen. George Crook from Fort Fetterman in Wyoming Territory, another under Col. John Gibbon from Fort Ellis in Montana Territory, and the third under Gen. Alfred Terry from Fort Abraham Lincoln in Dakota Territory. These troops were to converge on the main body of the Indians situated in southeastern Montana under the leadership of Sitting Bull, Crazy Horse, and other chiefs. Crook's troops were eliminated early, forced to withdraw from the campaign after clashing with a large Sioux–Cheyenne continent along the Rosebud River. The other two contingents, under Terry and Gibbon, met on the Yellowstone River near the mouth of the Rosebud. Terry then ordered Custer and the Seventh Cavalry, which were under his command, up the Rosebud to approach the Big Horn from the south. The rest of Terry's forces were to accompany Gibbon back up the Yellowstone and Big Horn Rivers to attack from the north.

Custer erred, most significantly in underestimating the size and fighting power of the Indians. He divided his

Maj. Marcus A. Reno, one of Custer's officers, had been dispatched with three battalions to attack the Sioux village from a different direction and thus escaped the fateful Last Stand on that June day in 1876.

Reno's troops and those of Capt. Frederick Benteen gathered in these bluffs where they were held to defensive actions by the Sioux.

600 men into three battalions, retaining five companies himself and assigning three each to Maj. Marcus Reno and Capt. Frederick Benteen. A twelfth was left to guard the pack train.

Benteen's orders were to scout the bluffs to the south, while Custer and Reno proceeded to the Indian village in the valley of the Little Big Horn. The latter two units seperated near the river. Reno was quickly outflanked and forced to retreat. Meeting up with Benteen, he and the captain went in search of Custer, who by then was somewhere in the north. But Reno and Benteen were again surrounded by Indians and forced to withdraw. Custer, meanwhile, found his command surrounded. In a vicious battle, the Seventh Cavalry was decimated as the entire contingent of five companies under Custer—about 210 men—was wiped out. Fifty-three men in Reno and Benteen's commands were killed and 60 wounded. The Indians probably suffered no more than 100 casualties.

The Custer Battlefield National Monument, which commemorates the devastating defeat that became known as Custer's Last Stand, lies within the Crow Indian Reservation in southeastern Montana. A battlefield tour begins at the Reno-Benteen site, four-and-a-half miles from the park's Visitor Center and continues to Custer Hill, from which the battlefield and the valley in which the Indian village was located can be seen. On the west side of the hill just below the monument, a grouping of 52 markers shows where Custer's battalion gathered for the "last stand." Custer, his brothers Tom and Boston, and his nephew were among those who fell here. The national cemetery holds the unidentified remains of soldiers and the identified body of Lt. John C. Crittenden. Soldiers killed in other Indian battles on the Northern Plains are also buried here.

This photo shows Medicine Tail Ford, where the Sioux were encamped at the time of the battle. The Little Big Horn River can be seen in the distance.

BIG HOLE BATTLEFIELD

WISDOM, MONTANA

(above) The Nez Perce pitched their 89 tipis on the east side of the Big Hole River, a grassy area that seemed perfect for a campsite. A day later, it was a battlefield.

(opposite) Prior to the battle, Col. John Gibbon had placed his howitzer on the ridge above the siege area. During the engagement, the Indians captured the field gun and rolled it down the hill.

The Battle of the Big Hole, which took place on August 9 and 10, 1877, marked a turning point in the war between the Nez Perce Indians and the U.S. army.

Early that summer, five Nez Perce bands, representing about 800 people, including about 125 warriors, began an arduous journey at the eastern tip of Oregon. They traversed through the Idaho Territory and over the Bitterroot Mountains into Montana Territory, bringing with them whatever possessions they could carry plus about 2,000 horses. They finally stopped at Bear's Paw Mountain in Montana, just south of the Canadian border. Despite the difficult terrain, they covered the distance in less than four months. Their motivation? The U.S. army was hot on their trail, under orders to place them on a reservation in western Idaho Territory.

The Indians had hoped to escape from the army without conflict, but this was not to be. On almost a dozen occasions, they had to stop and face their pursuers in the Nez Perce Indian War of 1877.

The problems started back at mid-century. Prior to that, the Nez Perce (named for the pierced noses that, according

This feather marks the spot where one of the Nez Perce was killed during the 24-hour engagement.

In mid-May 1877, General O. O. Howard gave the Nez Perce living off of the reservation 30 days to move onto the designated lands, threatening punitive action against those who did not comply.

to the French-Canadian trappers, some of the women sported; tribal members say their noses were never pierced) had made their traditional home in the area where what is now Oregon, Washington, and Idaho meet. Although the Nez Perce fought with other tribes, the area was a relatively quiet and serene environment until the settlers and gold miners began to arrive in large numbers. Still, in 1855, the Nez Perce signed a treaty that confined them to a reservation, an area that included much of their ancestral land.

By 1863, the continuing influx of settlers and traders in the area resulted in a new treaty. This time, the Nez Perce reservation was reduced to a quarter of its original size. The chiefs whose lands lay within the diminished area signed the agreement, but a third of the tribe lived outside the newly designated boundaries and consequently refused to abide by its strictures. Instead they remained in their homeland for several years, until an ever-increasing demand for settlement and mining land led the Indian Bureau to order them onto the smaller reservation. In mid-May 1877, General O. O. Howard gave this band 30 days to move. Indian leaders objected to the short notice, saying they couldn't comply until the fall. Howard ignored their protests, however, and threatened to strip the tribe of its horses and cattle if its members were not on the reservation within the prescribed time limit.

The chiefs reluctantly agreed to obey the order. The transition period was going smoothly until June 15, when three young warriors attacked and killed a group of white settlers to avenge the murder of several members of their families. Fearing army retaliation, the non-reservation Indians fled to nearby White Bird Camp. The soldiers attacked, but the Nez Perce beat them back.

For a month, the Nez Perce kept on the move as General Howard, facing increasing public pressure, attempted to round them up. On July 11, his forces finally caught up with the elusive Indians, this time near the Clearwater River. After a two-day battle, neither side could subdue the other. Finally, the Indians withdrew from the field, realizing that it was only a matter of time until Howard's forces defeated them. Thus began their long trek, which by early August found them in Montana. General Howard was far behind but Col. John Gibbon of the

Chief Joseph

Born in 1840, Chief Joseph was reared by both Protestant missionaries and his father, a leading chief of one of the richest Nez Perce tribes. By the time he had reached his adult years, Joseph was committed to peace with the whites, a commitment that he found increasingly difficult to sustain as his band's ancestral land was taken away from it by the U.S. government. In 1863, young Joseph faced a most difficult chore—conferring with white officials to dispute the contention that all Nez Perce, even those not subject to existing treaties, had to move onto reservations. He became a full chief in 1871, upon his father's death, urging his fellow chiefs to adopt humane rules in case of war.

Joseph was not a leading chief of the Nez Perce. He wasn't even a war chief. Rather, he was a civil chief whose authority rested on his devotion to duty and to principle. But his people recognized him as a dignified and calm guardian in a time of extreme need. His moment of greatest triumph came in 1877, as he zigzagged across the country with about 700 fellow tribe members, fleeing government forces who were intent upon putting them on the reservation. The press went so far as to call the 6-foot-2 inch, 200-pound chief "an Indian Napoleon."

In August 1877, soldiers attacked the Nez Perce on the east bank of the Big Hole River. During the initial charge, Joseph saved the life of his infant daughter, then helped to regroup the tribe, and to rally his people for a counterattack. Two months after the battle, the Nez Perce surrendered. Handing over his rifle, Joseph spoke the words that became his legacy: "Hear me, my chiefs. I am tired; my heart is sick and sad. From where the sun now stands, I will fight no more forever."

In 1904, 30 years after the battle, Chief Joseph died. Although he still expressed no animosity toward the white men, a reservation doctor diagnosed his ailment as a broken heart.

Chief Joseph, dubbed "an Indian Napoleon" by the press.

Seventh U.S. Infantry was now tracking them as well.

The tribe set up camp at Big Hole Valley, pitching 89 tipis, playing games, and relaxing. Believing themselves to be out of danger, they appointed no sentries. The next afternoon, Gibbon's men found the camp. Shortly before dawn on August 9, the 800 Nez Perce were awakened by gunfire. The soldiers and volunteers had rushed the camp, and ordered to fire at the first sight of Indians, they had begun shooting point blank at anyone they saw, killing men, women, and children—even infants—without discrimination. The Nez Perce rallied, killing a number of soldiers in return and forcing Gibbon to call a retreat. They also found good sniping positions, and used them to push the soldiers back across the river. There, Gibbon's men were pinned down for almost 24 hours, while the Nez Perce quickly broke camp, and moved southward.

The Nez Perce had won the Battle of the Big Hole but it did them little good. The army continued its pursuit and two months later the tribe was forced to surrender at the Battle of Bear's Paw Mountains.

The Big Hole National Battlefield is ten miles west of Wisdom, Montana. Visitors can tour the battlefield, and see the Nez Perce camp where the soldiers surprised the sleeping Indians. Also marked is the Siege Area where soldiers were held at bay for nearly 24 hours. The Howitzer Site marks the spot where the Nez Perce managed to capture the army's field gun, along with 2,000 rounds of ammunition. A videotape covering the battle and a museum are located at the Visitors Center.

A streak of red dramatically cuts a swath through the sky, as the sun sets on the Big Hole Battlefield.

(above) During the 1960s, a re-creation of Fort Hall was undertaken, based upon a set of plans of the original outpost supplied by Hudson's Bay Company. Fort Hall had been initially established in 1834 by Nathaniel Jarvis Wyeth.

(opposite) In the vicinity of Fort Hall were several hundred Bannock and Shoshone Indians willing to trade with the white men. Their presence helped insure the post's economic prosperity during its early days.

Old Fort Hall came into being as the result of a bungled business deal. For years, a sheltered part of Idaho's Snake River had been a favorite camping and gathering place for the Shoshone–Bannock Indians. But the large numbers of game and furbearing animals in the area also attracted the interest of white hunters and traders. In 1810, two representatives of the Missouri Fur Company visited the region, followed the next year by members of John Jacob Astor's Pacific Fur Company. Independent hunters and trappers soon appeared, as did members of the North West Company's Horse Brigade.

Through the 1820s and well into the 1830s, these and other fur companies continued their expeditions. An enterprising young businessman from New England named Nathaniel Jarvis Wyeth also became interested in the trading possibilities of the Pacific Northwest. In 1832, he made his first trip to the area, meeting trappers, traders, and Indians at an annual rendezvous. He also signed an agreement with representatives of the Rocky Mountain Fur Company, headquartered in St. Louis, to bring $3,000 in trade goods to them at the rendezvous two years later.

The factor's quarters were well furnished for an outpost in the 1830s and 1840s. They featured animal skins for rugs and mounted hunting trophies for decoration.

Wyeth arrived with the goods, but the company, in dire financial straights by then, refused the shipment. The entrepreneur, stuck with his merchandise, decided to move West with his men and sell the supplies himself. On July 15, 1834, he reached the Bottoms of the Snake River. Three days later, he began construction of a trading post. It was named Fort Hall in honor of the oldest member of the New England company financing his operation. The log structure was finished on August 4; the next day, Wyeth raised a homemade United States flag on the site and saluted it with a volley of shots.

Wyeth left Fort Hall on August 6, 1834, continuing his westward travels. He felt the future of the trading post was secure, the presence of several

The fort's sleeping quarters and storehouses were made of sturdy Idaho logs.

hundred Bannock and Shoshone Indians and their families camped in the area a good sign. He was wrong.

The Hudson's Bay Company was determined to put the upstart out of business. They built a trading post of their own, Fort Boise, near the place where the Boise River met the Snake. The HBC had almost limitless resources, enabling the company to overbid Wyeth in the payment of furs and underbid him in the sale of goods to the Indians. The strategy worked. Wyeth was unable to realize a decent profit from his post and, in 1837, sold out to the HBC. His reported loss was $30,000.

Perhaps if Wyeth could have held out a bit longer his luck would have changed, for in the early 1840s, thousands of emigrants headed West on the Oregon Trail and many of them stopped at Fort Hall. The early parties tended to abandon their wagons and some of their heavier possessions near the fort, convinced that the remainder of the trip could not be made on such conveyances. Then in 1843, a band of 875 emigrants refused to continue their journey without their wagons. They traveled safely on to the Dalles on the Columbia River, and by their example further opened development of the West.

After 1849, the HBC began to lose interest in Fort Hall. Profits were down and hostilities between white settlers and the neighboring Indian tribes was an increasing problem. Both Fort Hall and Fort Boise were abandoned in late 1855 and early 1856, and they fell into disrepair. Eventually, their remnants were removed for the construction of other buildings. Even the location of Fort Hall was forgotten.

Early in the 20th century, Ezra Meeker became concerned about the loss of sites that had dotted the Oregon Trail. To rectify the situation, he traveled to Washington, helped identify

The Oregon Trail

Of all the routes taken by traders, settlers, soldiers, missionaries, and gold seekers to traverse the West, none was as important as the Oregon Trail. For 20 years, this passageway was used by some 12,000 emigrants to travel the 2,000 miles from western Missouri to Oregon's Willamette River Valley and other areas in the Pacific Northwest.

The trail began in Independence, Missouri, extended across the Snake and Platte River Valleys, and ended at the mouth of the Columbia River. It was officially surveyed in 1841, after Missouri Senator Thomas Hart Benton, a firm believer in western expansionism, arranged for Congress to appropriate $30,000 for an expedition to find a viable pathway to the Pacific. John Charles Frémont, Benton's son-in-law, was named to head the expedition. Frémont's instructions were specific—to leave from Fort Leavenworth on the Missouri River, travel to the central Rockies paying specific attention to the topography of the South Pass, which was recognized as the gateway to Oregon, and then return home. The journey lasted from June until October and was a rousing success, resulting in a widely read report by Frémont who became known as the Pathfinder. In 1843, the first wagon train of settlers made its way along the trail, led by Peter Burnett, a Missouri lawyer. They were followed by such a flood of emigrants that in 1846 England was forced to relinquish her claims to Oregon. Thereafter, the territory became the sole possession of the United States, ultimately yielding the states of Oregon, Washington, and Idaho, as well as parts of Wyoming and Montana.

The trail today is marked by 125 historic sites. Among them are several forts, including the Fort Hall Recreation, that had been established at strategic points along the way to provide supplies and rest stops for the intrepid folk traveling West.

An artist's depiction of the Barlow Cutoff around Mount Hood on the Oregon Trail.

(top left) A lithograph published by the Baltimore firm of E. Weber & Co. in 1850 shows several Indians looking very much at home at Fort Hall.

(left) During the early 1840s, thousands of emigrants heading West on the Oregon Trail stopped at Fort Hall for supplies. The early parties tended to abandon their wagons near the fort, convinced that the remainder of the arduous trip could not be made on such conveyances.

(*above*) The company hall provided post residents with a spacious area for dining and relaxation. During the height of the trading season, as many as 20 people might be living on the premises.

strategic points along the trail, and set up markers to preserve their location. His efforts became the forerunner of what is the Oregon–California Trails Association. In 1916, a pair of doctors, inspired by Meeker perhaps, set out to find the fort's site. One of their company, a Native American named Joe Rainey, located what was believed to

be the spot, although some maintain it was actually an old stage station. In 1962, the construction of a replica began. The site that Rainey found could not be acquired, so the recreation was built on the upper level of Ross Park, 20 miles north of Pocatello, Idaho. It now houses interpretative displays, artifacts, and pioneer equipment.

(above) Fort Clatsop, Lewis and Clark's quarters during the winter of 1805, was a simple log stockade, made from the thick growth of pine that grew freely in the surrounding area.

(opposite) The enlisted men's quarters at the fort housed some 40 members of the Lewis and Clark party, who slept in rather roughly constructed bunk beds and used even tree stumps for furnishings.

Fort Clatsop exists due to the efforts of the famous explorers Meriwether Lewis and William Clark. The pair had been instructed by President Thomas Jefferson to explore lands acquired by the United States from France in the Louisiana Purchase. Specifically, Lewis and Clark were to trace the Missouri River to its source, establish the most direct land route to the Pacific, and make scientific and geographic observations along the way. At the same time, they were directed to study the Indian tribes they encountered and to impress upon the Native Americans the authority and power of the United States.

On May 14, 1804, the journey began at the mouth of the Missouri River near St. Louis. Forty-five men left civilization behind in a 55-foot keelboat and two smaller boats called *pirogues*. After traveling for five grueling months, they wintered at Fort Mandan, an outpost that they built among the Mandan Indian villages some 1,600 miles up the Missouri. There Toussaint Charbonneau, a half-breed interpreter, joined the expedition, along with his Shoshone wife, Sacagawea, and their infant son.

In April, 1805, the group resumed its journey, traveling by water almost to the source of the Missouri, and then by

The Louisiana Purchase

President Thomas Jefferson was an avowed Francophile, but he was nonetheless concerned about the return of Louisiana to France. Ceded to Spain during the French and Indian War, the territory, which included the post city of New Orleans, had remained for decades in the hands of the Spanish who had allowed Americans to traverse the Mississippi River as they wished. U.S. merchants were even able to store their goods duty free in New Orleans warehouses while they awaited shipment to Europe. Then, in 1800, the Spanish agreed by the Treaty of San Ildefonso to return Louisiana to France and suddenly America faced a real threat to its commerce—the replacement of the laissez-faire Spanish with the empire-minded Bonapartists. Even before the French resumed control of their lands, the port of New Orleans was closed to U.S. shipping. Something, Jefferson believed, had to be done.

What the president decided to do was buy the city of New Orleans and the land known as Florida from France, getting Congress to authorize a $2 million appropriation to that end. He then dispatched Robert Livingston, the U.S. minister to France, to negotiate with First Consul Bonaparte.

Unknown to Jefferson, Napoleon had troubles of his own, not the least of which was a slave revolt in Haiti. With a war against Great Britain imminent and faced with a shortage of funds, Napoleon met Livingston's offer to purchase New Orleans and Florida with an inquiry of his own: what would the U.S. pay for the whole Louisiana Territory? Dumbfounded, Liv-ingston had no idea but, after consulting with one of Jefferson's close friends and advisers, James Monroe, he offered Napoleon 50 million francs—and agreed to 60 million, about $15 million dollars.

Thus, with a stroke, the territory of the United States had been doubled and the land that would eventually form 13 states acquired at a price of about four cents an acre. In his haste to consumate the purchase—for fear of Napoleon's changing his mind—Jefferson believed that he had dramatically exceeded his authority. After all, Congress had only authorized the purchase of a small portion of the Louisiana Territory and had only allocated $2 million. Ironically, then, the president who had always opposed the concept of a strong chief executive became the one to significantly extend the powers of the presidency.

Six months earlier, Lewis and Clark had begun their celebrated exploration of the frontier. What had begun as a scientific excursion into the wilderness took on new meaning with the Louisiana Purchase, for the lands that these intrepid explorers were charting had become America's own.

Thomas Jefferson, third president of the United States and instigator of the Louisiana Purchase.

(above) Co-leader of the expedition, 33-year-old William Clark saved the exploring party from disaster on several occasions. An Indian fighter and professional soldier, he also served as the team's mapmaker and artist.

(above right) The other co-leader, Meriwether Lewis, had been a captain in the army prior to becoming President Jefferson's private secretary in 1801. Twenty-nine at the time of the expedition, he studied botany, zoology, and celestial navigation to prepare himself for the wilderness journey.

horseback over the Continental Divide. When they reached Idaho's Clearwater River, the men built more canoes which they used to travel 600 miles down the Snake and Columbia rivers before sighting the Pacific Ocean in November, 1805, near present-day McGowan, Washington. An entry from Lewis and Clark's journal dated November 7, 1805, reads: "Great joy . . . we are in view of the ocean . . . which we have been so long anxious to see, and the roaring or noise made by the waves breaking on the rocky shores . . . may be heard distinctly."

After ten days, Lewis and Clark decided to leave their camp on the north shore and cross the Columbia River to the south side where elk were reportedly plentiful. Scouting ahead, Lewis found a suitable site for a winter shelter, evidence of enough game for survival, and a salt supply. On December 8, 1805, the explorers began to build a fort about three miles up the Netal Creek (now the Lewis and Clark River). They were sheltered by Christmas Eve. The base of the fort, which was named for the friendly local Indian

Most of the activities at Fort Clatsop centered around the captains' quarters, where Meriwether Lewis and William Clark worked and reworked their maps and journals.

tribe, the Clatsops, featured a log stockade 50 feet square, located in a thick growth of pine. Inside, two rows of cabins were separated by a parade ground.

Much of the activity at the fort centered around the captains' quarters, occupied by Lewis and Clark. The pair worked constantly on their maps and journals and saw to the day-to-day management of the fort. Based on information provided by the Indians, they discovered that the route by which they had come was not the easiest and they decided to alter their plans for the return trip.

Indians came to the fort almost daily, both to visit and to trade. Lewis and Clark often wrote about the tribes, their skill in trading, their appearance, habits, living conditions, and abilities as hunters and fishermen. Much of the current knowledge about these indige-

nous peoples comes from Lewis and Clark's written observations.

Life at the fort was difficult, even for these seasoned explorers. All of the men hunted and trapped to keep food supplies up but, as spring approached, the elk took to the hills and it became increasingly difficult for members of the expedition to find meat and hides for food and clothing.

The weather also conspired against them. It rained for all but 12 of the 106 days spent at Fort Clatsop. Sleeping was difficult and soon almost every person was suffering from a cold or rheumatism. Despite the hardships, it was a most worthwhile expedition. Every member of the team could claim a place in history as a great explorer.

The reconstructed fort illustrates many of the frontier skills employed by Lewis and Clark during the winter of 1805/06. In the summer, National Park Service rangers demonstrate canoe building, hide tanning, and the use of flintlock firearms.

The intrepid members of the Lewis and Clark expedition learned a host of new skills, many of them from the Native Americans they encountered. Here, a costumed interpreter at the fort carves out an impressive canoe.

FORT NISQUALLY

TACOMA, WASHINGTON

(*above*) During the 1840s, large storehouses became necessary at the fort, as almost 1,000 acres of the surrounding land were under cultivation.

(*opposite*) In 1849, Indians attacked the fort, killing an American settler and injuring two others. It was the only violent incident between whites and Native Amricans during Nisqually's history.

It was spring 1832, when Archibald MacDonald, chief fur trader for Hudson's Bay Company, took a fairly routine trip between two of the British firm's outposts, Fort Langley and Fort Vancouver. He paused for a few days on the lower Puget Sound region, just north of the Nisqually River. Having received instructions to establish a post in this vicinity, he supervised the construction of a storehouse and left several servants in charge of it. These hapless few were given a couple of kegs of potatoes, some garden seeds, and a few blankets for trade.

The next year, MacDonald was again traveling the region, this time with an entourage of Hudson's Bay Company employees and a doctor. The party stopped at "Nisqually House"—the storehouse that MacDonald had established in 1832—and decided to construct a larger, enclosed fortification nearby. The new site, one mile from the beach location of Nisqually House, was named Fort Nisqually. According to one theory, the name derives from the term "squally," which the local tribes used to describe the tall prairie grass as it blew in the wind.

MacDonald stayed at Fort Nisqually long enough to supervise the construction and then made his way north.

Dr. William Tolmie, the physician who had been traveling with MacDonald's entourage, was left behind when a worker accidentally cut himself with an ax. He remained at Nisqually until the following year, a time during which the fort was under the direction of chief trader Francis Heron.

In May 1834, William Kittson began his six-and-a-half year administration of the fort. At this time, the post consisted of four buildings and pickets so flimsy that they would blow down in a strong wind. Kittson soon had the company servants, as well as the Indian employees, alter the houses within the 100-foot-square compound so that the doors faced toward the center, thus providing their own windbreak.

Kittson ran a successful operation. Beaver, the most common pelt harvested by the Indians, was so plentiful it had to be shipped back to Great Britain each year in 90-pound bales. And trade conditions were favorable. The local tribes particularly valued the company's blankets. One of these rather common textiles brought two large beaver pelts in return. The price of a trade gun averaged 22 pelts. When the fur trade began to decline in the 1830s, the company decided to direct its efforts elsewhere. As early as 1834, cattle from Mexican California had been introduced to Fort Nisqually and had flourished. In 1839, Dr. John McLoughlin, chief factor at Fort Vancouver, decided to launch the Puget Sound Agricultural Company and make Fort Nisqually its main station. Work proceeded at a furious pace, with post administrator Alexander Caulfield Anderson spending much of 1840 on horseback, collecting sheep and cattle. Eventually, the fort's future in the hide and tallow business was assured. In time, Fort Nisqually would come to supply all of the posts of the Hudson's Bay Company on the Pacific coast with grain, butter, beef, cheese, wool, mutton, and hides.

In 1843, chief trader Dr. William Tolmie, returning from a spell in England, began his 16-year tenure as administrator of the fort. These were times of change for Nisqually, with Tolmie even uprooting the entire operation and moving it one mile inland in order to be closer to the water supply and to obtain more open acreage for farming and livestock production. The new fort was built in the same format as the old, with the center of operations for the Puget Sound Agricultural Company serving as the nucleus around which the other structures were erected. The operation claimed 252 square miles with another 1,000 acres under cultivation at times.

Nisqually's troubles began in 1846, when the long-disputed American border with Canada was set at the 49th parallel. This put the British outpost in U.S. territory. American settlers began

(left) **Dr. William Tolmie, the fort's first doctor, had been touring various Hudson's Bay Company installations when a worker at Nisqually accidentally cut himself with an ax. Tolmie remained at the outpost until the following year.**

(right) **From the wide veranda of the factor's house, a "trapper" surveys the compound of the fort built in 1833.**

(above) The factor's house at Fort Nisqually featured two bedrooms, a dining hall, a parlor, and a hallway, quite an extravagant structure for a Pacific Northwest outpost during the fur-trade era.

(left) Archibald MacDonald, chief fur trader for Hudson's Bay Company, established Fort Nisqually in 1833.

to flood into the area, encroaching upon company land. Often, they stole company cattle as well. Tolmie sent for the British navy, which arrived in Nisqually Bay with armed battleships in case violence broke out. The Indians also felt the pressure of the newcomers' presence and, in 1849, attacked the fort, apparently failing to distinguish between the English company employees and the American pioneers. In the attack, an American settler was killed and two others injured, the only violent incident between whites and Native Americans during Nisqually's history. Eventually, the injustices against the company and its property became so severe that a settlement of claims between the HBC and the United States was reached and Tolmie left the area.

Fort Nisqually was relocated to Point Defiance Park, in Tacoma, Washington, in the 1930s. The re-created fort shows the site as it was in the years 1843–1859. Some 12 structures have been erected, including the factor's house, the granary, the men's dwelling house, and the stockade.

Mountain Men

Modern definitions of "macho" should include some reference to mountain men, a group of tough fur trappers who spilled through the Rocky Mountains from early in the 19th century to about 1840. Their search for beaver led them into remote regions of the West, places no white person had ever seen before. They discovered salt lakes and geysers of steam, fought wild animals, and, in general, lived lives so rough that their reports couldn't be discussed in genteel company. According to some accounts, the first mountain man was John Colter. A member of Lewis and Clark's 1806 expedition up the Missouri, he decided to return to the western wilderness at the end of that epic journey and consequently spent the next four years living in the wild, an existence of unbelievable hardship and brutality. The Virginian set an example for other men, stimulating them to compete for the fur trade in the West. Among those who followed in Colter's footsteps were the legendary Kit Carson, Jim Baker, and Jim Bridger, who used what they learned in the wild to later become army scouts and wagon train guides. Surprisingly, Baker and Bridger ended their careers as farmers in Wyoming and Missouri respectively.

The mountain men were both rogues and heroes. They made their own rules and lived their lives accordingly. They were usually poorly equipped, even by the standards of the time. The men usually dressed in buckskin and carried one extra set of leggings. Typically, their baggage consisted of knives, a pipe and tobacco, a gun, powder and lead, and perhaps some reading material. Little food was transported, as a mountain man lived almost exclusively off of the land. His guns were his most prized possessions, with his beaver traps a close second.

Legendary mountain man, scout, and wagon train guide, Jim Baker.

Tyee House was one of the first buildings to be constructed at Fort Nisqually. Today, it is one of 15 structures that stand within the post's compound.

(left) The interior of Tyee House. Until construction of the factor's house, it served as the residence and the office for the post's manager.

(below) In the granary, animal skins drape the top of a typical Hudson's Bay Company shipping crate. Beaver, the most common pelt harvested by the Indians, was so plentiful in the area that it was annually shipped back to Great Britain in 90-pound bales.

(opposite) The fort's bastions, one of which is seen in the background of this photo, were built slowly over a period of years. Ironically, Indian attacks periodically interrupted the work. The structure to the right is Storehouse #2.

FORT VANCOUVER

VANCOUVER, WASHINGTON

(above) The chief factor's residence, which replaced an earlier, less imposing structure, featured such refinements as white clapboard siding and a large veranda.

(opposite) A closeup of the kitchen building, with a cordon of firewood stacked up to the height of the window.

For two decades, the stockaded fur-trading post of Fort Vancouver served as the Columbia Department headquarters for Britain's Hudson's Bay Company. It served a region encompassing present-day British Columbia, Washington, Oregon, and Idaho. The trading post also represented Britain's business and governmental interests during a period when the United Kingdom and the United States engaged in a fierce battle for control over the fur-rich region. Given these roles, Fort Vancouver became the nucleus of the early development of the Pacific Northwest and an economic, cultural, political, and social hub.

Fort Vancouver traces its origins to 1824, when the Hudson's Bay Company decided to move its headquarters from Fort George at the mouth of the Columbia River to a site about 100 miles upstream. The transfer was made for two reasons. First, it was seen as a way to strengthen British claims to the territory north of the Columbia. Second, it allowed proximity to better farmland. The new post was named Fort Vancouver, in honor of explorer Capt. George Vancouver.

For two decades, the fort was directed by two powerful men who built it into the fur trade capital of the Pacific

Hudson's Bay Company

In 1763, the British conquered Canada and inherited a rich fur trade, which they capitalized on by forming two companies: the North West Company, which opened up the Canadian West, and the Hudson's Bay Company, an Eastern-based firm that enjoyed the patronage of the British crown. As early as 1803, President Thomas Jefferson expressed concern about the power of these firms, suggesting that it was American interests that should flourish beyond the Mississippi. Those Indians who sold exclusively to the British-based companies, said Jefferson, should be enticed to sell to the Americans instead. Although he was careful to avoid any suggestion of military aggression against the British, he did argue for means that would extend "the external commerce of the U.S."

In 1821, the North West Company joined with Hudson's Bay. The new entity, usually called HBC, which wags claimed stood for "Here Before Christ," seemed inviolate, controlling a fur-trading area that was immense. In 1825, the HBC moved its headquarters in the Oregon Territory to the newly established Fort Vancouver, 100 miles upstream. For 20 years, Fort Vancouver served as the fur-trading capital of the coastal region. With the support of the British govern-

ment, the HBC was always able to underbid any upstart American trader who might get in the way.

In 1846, the Oregon Territory was divided between the U.S. and the British along the 49th parallel, leaving Fort Vancouver on American soil. Thereafter, HBC trade diminished, forcing the company to abandon the post in 1860. Other outposts were also vacated. Fort Hall, where the company banner had been flying since 1837, saw the British depart in 1855.

The Hudson's Bay Company is still vital in Canada, where it is the country's oldest existing company. During the course of its 320-year history, it has moved from fur trading to frontier real estate to shops, pausing along the way to invest in a Scotch whiskey distillery and various resource companies. Today, it is best known for its department stores.

Employees of the Hudson's Bay Company on their annual expedition.

coast. Dr. John McLoughlin, commander of Fort Vancouver from 1824–1846, was a Canadian-born and trained physician, who joined the North West Company as a doctor for its post at Fort William (near present-day Thunder Bay, Ontario). When the North West and Hudson's Bay companies merged, McLoughlin was named head of the Columbia Department. Known to the Indians as White Eagle, he kept peace with various tribes, effectively squeezed the Americans out of the market, and established the British claim to all of the Oregon Territory. Thanks largely to his efforts, the firm's Columbia Department was expanded until it stretched from the Rockies to the Pacific, and from Russian Alaska to Mexican California, with outposts on San Francisco Bay and in Hawaii.

Sir George Simpson was head of North American operations for the Hudson's Bay Company and the man who hired John McLoughlin. While he admired the latter's administrative skills and leadership ability, Simpson never really liked his subordinate. During the fort's existence, the enmity between the two men was evident.

Fort Vancouver was the focal point for a vast commercial empire. Here, the furs of the company's entire western trade were gathered each year for shipment to England. The post was also an important farming and manufacturing community. Its location allowed for a supply of lumber, pickled salmon, and other products from its mills, drying sheds, and forges, some of which were traded to such remote locations as the Hawaiian Islands and Alaska. The fort was also a cultural center, home to the Oregon Territory's first school, first circulating library, first theater, and one of the earliest churches in the Northwest.

At its most prosperous, in the years between 1844 and 1846, Fort Vancouver was a massive establishment. The fort proper measured approximately 732 feet by 325 feet and was surrounded by a stockade of upright logs, with a bastion in one corner mounting cannons. The defenses were not

(above) Fort Vancouver, constructed in 1824, measured 732 feet by 325 feet. It was surrounded by a stockade of upright logs, with a bastion at the northwest corner.

(left) The Indian Trade Shop stocked a wide variety of goods, including the company's blankets, which were particularly valued by the tribes of the region. One of these rather common textiles brought two large beaver pelts in return.

necessary, as the nearby Indians weren't hostile and the area's American settlers never went beyond verbal threats. There were 22 major buildings within the compound, and several lesser structures. The former included a jail, four large storehouses, an Indian tradeshop, and impressive dwellings for company officers and clerks. The lesser employees of the fort lived in a village on the plain west and southwest of the complex.

During the 1830s and 1840s, American settlers were attracted to the rich farmland of Oregon. John McLoughlin's hospitality and kind treatment made their lives easier, and they came to the British outpost for supplies of food, seeds, and farm implements. McLoughlin retired from the Hudson's Bay Company in 1846, moved to Oregon City, and became a U.S. citizen. Today he is known as the "Father of Oregon."

That same year, 1846, the United States and Great Britain signed a treaty that made Fort Vancouver part of American territory. A rapid decline in Fort Vancouver's fortunes occurred, as the British post and company were now operating on what was clearly defined as foreign soil and as settlers began to take over the land near the fort. Indeed, the company welcomed the protection afforded it in 1849 by the establishment of a U.S. Army camp nearby. Soon, a military reservation was created around the old fur-trading post and in 1860 it was officially handed over to the American army. Six years later, all traces of the original stockade were destroyed by fire.

The present Fort Vancouver is a reconstruction of the original, but the stockade and five major buildings sit on their original sites. Visitors can see the blacksmith's shop, the bakery, the Indian trade shop and dispensary, the wash house, kitchen, and the home of John McLoughlin.

Fort Vancouver was named in honor of explorer Capt. George Vancouver.

(right) The fort's kitchen, seen in the upper right in this photo, contained a cooking area, a pantry, a larder, and living quarters for some of the staff. The wash house to its left is a re-creation of the original, destroyed by fire in 1852.

(opposite) A pot heats on the raging fire in the kitchen hearth.

The Southwest

TRAVIS   CROCKETT

THE ALAMO

SAN ANTONIO, TEXAS

(above) Perhaps the most widely recognized battle site in the world, the Alamo today gives no hint of the 13-day siege that its occupants endured more than 150 years ago.

(opposite) The Alamo Monument stands as a tribute to the 183 freedom-fighters who lost their lives at the former mission on March 6, 1836.

(previous pages) The Presidio La Bahia in Goliad, Texas, the oldest fort in the western United States.

One of the most famous battle sites in the world had its beginnings as nothing more than a collection of crude huts on the San Pedro Creek in Texas. In 1718, San Antonio's first mission was built, a Spanish outpost intended to bring religion and "civilization" to the Indians of the area. It was moved to the east bank of the river, still a primitive collection of buildings, and destroyed by a hurricane in 1724. Three years later, a two-story stone structure had been started. Originally intended as a home for priests and a collection of offices, this edifice would later become known as the Long Barrack during the Texas Revolution. Work continued sporadically on the mission until 1793, when the clerical administration of the surrounding territory ceased and the priests were replaced by civil authorities.

The Spanish cavalry moved into the abandoned mission, occupying it until Mexican troops took it over in 1821. It was called the Alamo, after the occupying cavalry company, organized at El Alamo, a town in Coahuila, Mexico.

After Mexico won her independence from Spain, Texas sought hers from Mexico in 1835. Mexican Gen. Martin

Perfecto de Cos, who was sent to San Antonio to quell the rebellious Texans, converted the mission into a fortress, its thick stone and adobe walls making it secure. However, Perfecto de Cos was under a lengthy siege by Stephen Austin, leader of the Texas colony. Short of supplies and food, the Mexicans surrendered on December 10, 1835.

The president of Mexico, Gen. Antonio Lopez de Santa Anna, was enraged by the plucky Texans' actions and plotted his retaliation. He massed a huge army along the Rio Grande, vowing death to every rebel bearing arms.

By February 1836, the town was guarded by 150 men under the command of Col. William Barret Travis. They were a tough lot and included two men who were destined to become American legends. James Bowie, Louisiana sugar plantation owner and state legislator who fled to Texas after killing a man in a duel and Tennessean David Crockett, who had been a frontiersman, soldier, and a member of the United States Congress. The men defending San Antonio took refuge in the Alamo. They waited for reinforcements daily. When these failed to

Jim Bowie, commander of the volunteer militia at the Alamo, met his end in bed. He had fallen from a fortification prior to the battle on March 6, injuring his leg.

arrive, they were hopeful that volunteers from the United States would join them. Instead, Santa Anna arrived, ringing the Alamo with troops on February 23 and ordering the garrison to surrender or be put to the sword. In order to pursuade the rebels, he began a bombardment with light field pieces, a move that led Travis to put out his famous appeal for help to Texans and all Americans: "If this call is neglected, I am determined to sustain myself as long as possible and die like a soldier who never forgets what is due to his own honor and that of his country—Victory or Death!"

But only a small contingent—32 men and boys from Gonzales—made their way through the Mexican lines, bringing the number of defenders at the Alamo to 189. Fewer than 20 were citizens of Texas.

Col. William Barrett Travis was the commander of the regulars at the Alamo. In his stirring appeal for outside aid in the days preceeding the mission's fall, he called for "Victory or Death!"

The facade of the shrine, whose original construction commenced in 1727, features intricately carved stone walls and pillars and heavy wooden doors. While it is impressive, this ornamentation is relatively simple compared to the elaborate motifs employed by the Spanish in Mexico's principal cities.

Stephen Austin

In 1820, when Stephen Austin was a 26-year-old law student in New Orleans, his father, Moses, proposed that they apply to the Spanish rulers of Mexico for a large land grant in the Mexican colony of Texas—and then dole out acreage to American pioneers for profit. The scheme was a wild one, so absurd that the son resisted for a year before agreeing. His sense of filial obligation was to eventually earn him the nickname the "Father of Texas."

The Missouri natives went ahead with their plan. In May 1821, Moses got word from the authorities in Mexico that he would be granted 200,000 Texas acres of his choice. For his part, Moses promised to settle the land with 300 American families, all sympathetic to Spain. Moses died a month later but Stephen decided to carry out his father's plan alone. On July 15, 1821, he and a handful of Americans headed for San Antonio.

Austin ran himself ragged trying to start his colony off properly. The first few months were wretched, as provisions for the new settlement were slim. Then, in March 1822, Austin learned that the Mexicans had staged a revolution, ousted the Spanish, and nullified his land grant. He hurried to Mexico City and after nearly a year there won approval from the Mexican congress for his colony under very favorable terms. But there were two conditions—every settler had to become a Mexican citizen and every settler had to accept Roman Catholicism.

By 1825, the colony was so prosperous that Austin had created four districts, each with its own elected leader. In the next decade, Austin received several new land grants, bounties that only added to his exhausting work. He cared deeply for the settlers and was often frustrated by the resentment that they seemed to hold for him. Then, in 1833, the frustrated 39-year-old decided that Texas could no longer continue as a Mexican colony. He was arrested and held in prison for two years. But when he was released, he called for war with Mexico. And war it became. In the conflict, he lost everything but his life.

Following the Texans' victory and the declaration of the Lone Star Republic, Austin ran against Sam Houston for the nation's new presidency but lost badly, finishing the campaign humiliated and impoverished. Houston, however, named him Secretary of State and he died in 1837, honored by his fellow Texans, at the age of 43.

Stephen Austin, the Louisiana lawyer, who became known as the "Father of Texas."

Santa Anna had far greater luck with his reinforcements. Perhaps 3,000 men surrounded the adobe walls on March 6 when, a little before dawn, the Mexicans launched their attack. Bugles sounded the dreaded "deguello"—which literally meant that no prisoners were to be taken.

The carnage was horrid. The attackers fell but more kept coming. They swarmed the plaza and into the mission, as the Texans tried vainly to stop them, resorting even to hand-to-hand combat with knives and rifle butts to no avail. All but five defenders died in the brief engagement, and they were later executed. The bodies of the Texans were burned; the dead Mexicans (an estimated 600) were buried until the graveyard overflowed. A handful of those present in the Alamo were spared—women, children, and servants—who lived to tell the dreadful tale.

Today, the Alamo stands as a memorial to those who died. In addition to a shrine in the center of the grounds, there is the Long Barrack, the Alamo Museum, and a research library.

David Crockett, frontiersman and member of the United States Congress, died at the Alamo. A bust of the celebrated backwoodsman sits in the Long Barrack.

Initially intended to provide living quarters for the mission's priests, the Long Barrack subsequently saw life as a hospital and is now a museum.

Strolling along this shady walkway beside the Alamo, one can get a sense of the sturdy stone construction of the mission building.

(above) La Bahia, which means "the bay," was relocated to Goliad, Texas, in 1749 to serve as protector and bastion of the Spanish borderlands. It embattled Native Americans and the forces of other European nations for more than 100 years.

(opposite) Loretto Chapel features the only original example of Spanish Colonial "groin vault architecture" in the United States.

Presidio la Bahia had been established in 1721 among the ruins of a French outpost, Fort Saint Louis, on the Texas Gulf coast. Its name, La Bahia, literally means "the bay." It was relocated to its present site in the town of Goliad in 1749 when colonizer José Escandon established the military garrison on the San Antonio River. There, the fort served as protector and bastion of the Spanish borderlands, embattling Native Americans and the forces of other European nations for more than 100 years.

In February 1836, during Texas' fight for independence with Mexico, Texas colonist Col. James Walker Fannin had control of Presidio la Bahia. He and his 400 well-armed young recruits from the United States and Europe had decided to attack the Mexican town of Matamoros, 25 miles away. In the opinion of some, including Texas governor Henry Smith who opposed it, it was a reckless scheme.

Meanwhile, the Alamo, another outpost held by the rebels in nearby San Antonio came under the threat of attack. Although Col. James Neill, commander at the former mission church, had appealed for help to man his skimpy garrison, Fannin refused. He wanted to remain at

La Bahia, the only fully restored Spanish Colonial presidio in existence, has been reconstructed to conform to the fort's appearance in 1835/36.

Goliad, believing that he and his men could successfully carry off their invasion. He changed his mind, however, when the commander of the Texan forces, Sam Houston, visited the presidio and warned him that the Mexicans were indeed coming and that they were intent on quelling the rebellion. For the moment at least Fannin decided to stay put.

He then began to receive a series of increasingly desperate messages from the Alamo. Under the threat of imminent attack, the new commander, Lt. Col. William Travis, clearly expected support from the troops at Goliad, a mere 95 miles away. But Fannin instead decided to remain at the presidio, which had been renamed "Fort Defiance," and await a possible Mexican attack there.

After his victory at the Alamo on March 6, 1836, Mexican General Antonio Lopez de Santa Anna moved quickly in an effort to overwhelm what remained of the Texas forces. That same month, he ordered Gen. José Francisco Urrea to drive up from the south with 1,400 men and capture the Presidio la Bahia.

Meanwhile, Fannin had been ordered to destroy the fort, bury the heavy artillery, and retreat. He obeyed his instructions, setting out with his troops on March 19, but had traveled only nine miles on the open plain when he was set upon by two Mexican divisions under Urrea. Without sufficient ammunition, food, or protection, Fannin and his men surrendered after the Battle of Coleto on the 19th and 20th. They were taken prisoner by the Mexicans, and returned to the fort where they were used as servants, nurses, and doctors. They had no way of knowing Santa Anna had already ordered their execution.

On Palm Sunday, March 27, 1836, the men were marched outside the walls of the presidio. Most believed they were being assigned another work detail. Instead, their captors gunned them down. Fannin himself was shot in the head in the chapel courtyard.

Santa Anna

It is one of history's ironies that the man embraced by most Texans as their savior would later become their most hated enemy.

Born in Jalapa, Mexico, in 1794, Antonio Lopez de Santa Anna launched a military campaign to unseat Mexico's head of government, Anastacio Bustamente, in 1832. The Texans rushed to throw their support behind him, believing that he was the man who would understand their aspirations. They knew little about him, had no way of knowing that he was a womanizer, an opium eater, and so phobic about water that he could barely cross a river. To be sure, he was a skilled soldier, but he was also completely unprincipled, eager for fame, and hungry for wealth. The son of a minor colonial officer, he was to achieve many of his ambitions. The cost, however, would be high.

After assuming power in 1833, Santa Anna granted the Texans a number of reforms. Indeed, he gave them everything they wanted. Every-thing, that is, except statehood. Then he turned his attention to consolidating his power, creating a strong, centralized federal government with himself as its head. He also strengthened the military garrisons and put his brother-in-law, General Martin Perfecto de Cos, in charge of the eastern provinces, including Texas. Before long, Santa Anna had become a virtual dictator.

Texas' hopes for Mexico's president were soon dashed. Indeed, by mid-1835, when talk of war between Mexico and Texas was everywhere, Stephen Austin called him a "base, unprincipled monster." On October 2, 1835, the revolution began. Although his forces dramatically outnumbered those of the Texans, Santa Anna, who took the field against the rebels himself, was out-generaled by Sam Houston at the Battle of San Jacinto on April 21, 1836. Captured by the Texans, he was held prisoner until November, when he was released. Forced to retire from office, he regained power briefly in 1838, then took control of the government again two years later and ruled until he was driven into exile in 1845. He returned to Mexico when war with the United States erupted, having

Santa Anna, Mexico's president, fancied himself as the "Napoleon of the West."

convinced the American president, James K. Polk, that he would work for peace. Instead he led an army against the United States, which was defeated by Gen. Winfield Scott. This time he retired for good, first to Jamaica and then New Granada. He was allowed to return to his homeland in 1874, two years before he died. He was blind and penniless.

El Quartel, the enlisted men's barracks, was built in 1749. Constructed of limestone blocks, it housed approximately 30 men.

About 128 Texans managed to survive the massacre. Of these, about 30—doctors, artisans, and some wounded soldiers—were spared. Another 30 escaped into the nearby river marshes. Forty other injured men, too sick to take part in the death march, were killed separately at the fort. The Goliad Massacre, as the Texans called it, became, along with the Alamo, a symbol of Mexican repression.

The fort has now been restored, looking as it did under Fannin's command. Officers' quarters, the military chapel, the barracks, the guardhouse, and the bastions at each corner of the quadrangle have been rebuilt according to the original dimensions.

(right) La Bahia's Loretto Chapel is the oldest existing church on America's Gulf Coast. It was a military chapel, which distinguished it from the many missions that the Spanish built to house priests and convert Indians.

(below) Hailing from several of Georgia's most prominent families, planter Col. James Walker Fannin, Jr., was an early advocate of Texas independence. Killed in the Goliad Massacre, he was remembered in an oil painting by his cousin, Samuel F. B. Morse.

SAN JACINTO BATTLEFIELD

HOUSTON, TEXAS

(*above*) This aerial view shows the Mexican campsite, where a confident Santa Anna lay sleeping in his tent on April 20, 1836, when the Texans attacked.

(*opposite*) An intricate sundial sits in de Zavala Plaza, a modern monument to a historic battle.

The Battle of San Jacinto was over practically before it started. After a mere 18 minutes, the victor had been declared and the course of history altered. In that brief time span, 637 people were killed, 238 wounded, and the independence of Texas won.

On the night before the battle, the evening of April 20, 1836, Gen. Sam Houston, the commander in chief of the Texas forces, was a man under extreme duress. For weeks, he and his army had been on the retreat, declining to enter into battle with the Mexican army of Gen. Antonio Lopez de Santa Anna. While the Texas colonists watched in horror, Santa Anna had marched through the countryside, leaving in his wake a swath of death and destruction that included his victory at the Alamo in March. By April, the Mexican leader felt confident that he had demoralized all of Texas. To a degree, he was right. Houston's continued refusal to face Santa Anna's troops had led to calls for his resignation and charges of cowardice.

But Houston was waiting, biding his time while he trained his raw troops. He arrived on Buffalo Bayou, opposite Harrisburg, on April 18. The town was in ruins, burned to the ground by Santa Anna, who had hoped to capture David Burnet, the fleeing president of Texas, there. Houston learned that Santa Anna planned to proceed eight miles to Lynch's Ferry, the only viable way across the San Jacinto River. The Texan also learned that the main body of Mexican army had been left behind and that its leader was traveling with a relatively small contingent of men. The opportune moment had come.

Houston's men, between 783 to 900 in number, won the race to the ferry, arriving at dawn on April 20. A detail of Mexicans was already there, guarding a boat filled with provisions, but they fled when the Texans arrived. The famished army feasted on the captured rations. Soon after, Houston set up camp in a stand of timber skirting the Buffalo Bayou about a mile from the ferry crossing. The Mexicans arrived at noon and immediately attempted to draw the Texans into battle. Houston refused, content to let his two cannons engage in fire with Santa Anna's single fieldpiece. The seemingly fruitless duel continued even as Mexican reinforcements arrived. Houston went to bed, leaving strict orders he was not to be disturbed. He woke well after daylight on April 21, refreshed and energized. He still did nothing.

Santa Anna began to relax. Although his men were tired and he had been afraid of attack, the lack of activity seemed to be a good sign. Meanwhile, in Houston's camp, breakfast was being prepared. At 9 a.m., additional Mexican reinforcements arrived, 400–500 more men to add to the 750 already encamped. Santa Anna now had a numerical advantage over the Texans. Tension ebbed and he ordered his men to eat and rest. He was so confident that he did not even post a sentry.

While the Mexicans relaxed, Houston ordered the destruction of Vince's Bridge to prevent more of the enemy from arriving. At noon, he held his first and only council of war, followed by a parade assembly at 3:30, at which

The marker in the foreground distinguishes the grave of Lorenzo de Zavala, whose plantation served as a field hospital following the Battle of San Jacinto.

A simple stone marker commemorates the site of the greatest carnage during the battle. Shouting "Remember the Alamo!" the Texans, led by Sam Houston, defeated Santa Anna and his army in just 18 minutes.

(*above*) Called the treaty oak stump, this natural artifact marks the spot where Santa Anna met with Houston after the battle. The declaration that they signed here brought an end to the hostilities between Texas and Mexico.

(*left*) After months of avoiding the Mexican army, the Texans met the forces of Santa Anna at San Jacinto on April 21, 1836, and won independence for the Lone Star Republic.

Sam Houston

Sam Houston's ancestors arrived in the New World from Scotland in 1730 and eventually became wealthy Virginia plantation owners. Sam's father, who had little interest in farming, entered the military, leaving the plantation to gather debt. Thus, by the time Samuel Houston, Sr., died in 1806, the family had lost its money. When Sam Houston, Jr., was 14, his mother packed up her brood of nine children, left the plantation, and moved to Tennessee, clearing land for a farm. Three years later, at 17, Sam left home—and wandered into a nearby Cherokee camp. He was soon adopted by the chief of the tribe, who named him Co-lon-eh, or the Raven. Houston spent three years with the Cherokee, an idyllic time that ended in 1813.

Young Sam's return to the white world was sparked by word of a bloodthirsty tribe called the Red Sticks (a faction of the Creek Indians named for their crimson war clubs) who were on a rampage through Alabama. The United States forces were marching to end their violence, and Sam Houston decided to join them, fighting his first battle at the age of 20 under Gen. Andrew Jackson. The young man's courage was extraordinary: wounded three times, he continued to battle the enemy. Jackson never forgot young Houston's bravery.

In 1818, Sam resigned from the army, obtained a law degree, set up a practice, and began his astonishing political rise. He became attorney general of Tennessee in 1819, a commander of the Tennessee militia in 1821, and a U.S. congressman in 1823. By 1827, he was governor of his state and, a year later, his close friend, Andrew Jackson, became president.

Sam Houston set foot in Texas for the first time in 1833. He had survived charges of corruption in Congress, had assaulted a fellow member and been forgiven, and was ready for a new challenge. A presidential mission to Texas seemed the right idea. His presence was potent; his battles numerous. The most important of these, the Battle of San Jacinto, simply reaffirmed his courage. After Texas' independence had been won, he became president of the Lone Star Republic, and later, after Texas entered the Union, a U.S. senator.

He married twice, the first time briefly and unhappily; the second time in 1840, when he was 47, to a 21-year-old bride. Margaret and Sam had eight children in 17 years and were still married when he died of pneumonia in 1863. His final words were: "Texas—Texas—Margaret!"

Sam Houston, hero of San Jacinto, president of the Lone Star Republic, governor of the state of Texas, and U.S. senator.

he inspected his men, and deployed them into a battleline. Just after 4 p.m., the Texans moved slowly and silently toward the Mexican lines. The only advantage they possessed was surprise.

The Mexicans, meanwhile, were relaxing. Santa Anna was in fact asleep in his tent. With the Texans only 200 yards away, a soldier suddenly noticed the advancing army. Holding their fire until they were 60 yards away, the Texans charged, urged on by Houston, mounted on a white horse, shouting "Remember the Alamo! Remember the Alamo!" As the fierce battle broke out, much of it hand-to-hand combat, Houston's horse was shot out from under him; he immediately mounted another. Within 18 minutes, it was all over.

Sam Houston was injured, his right legbone shattered above the ankle. He nearly died in the following days from blood loss, exhaustion, and gangrene but he survived to become president of the Lone Star Republic. Santa Anna was taken prisoner the day after the battle and, although most Texans wanted him hanged, he was kept safe to be used by Houston to relieve Texas of enemy troops and thereby insure that there would be no future attacks against the Lone Star Republic.

Today, the 1,000-acre San Jacinto Battleground State Historical Park, located on the Houston Ship Channel near Houston, Texas, marks the significant points in the famous battle. A 570-foot high memorial commemorates the heroes of the engagement and all those who fought for the independence of Texas.

(opposite) The San Jacinto Monument was constructed in 1936–1939 to commemorate the heroes of the Battle of San Jacinto and all the other soldiers who helped Texas win its independence. The reinforced concrete structure stands 570 feet high and has a museum at its base.

FORT DAVIS

FORT DAVIS, TEXAS

(*above*) Officer's row consists of 13 one-story buildings, completed between 1869 and 1871. The first three were made of stone; the others were principally adobe. Although they look similar from the front, those occupied by higher ranking officers had additional rooms in the back.

(*opposite*) From the issue room of the commissary, seen here, enlisted men received their rations of flour, tobacco, and other staples. Officers, who weren't issued rations, could buy goods here, including such luxury items as canned salmon.

The Mexican War of 1846–1848 added a large new area to the United States, land that included the present-day states of New Mexico, Arizona, California, and Texas. When gold was discovered in California in 1848, westward overland travel routes became increasingly important as thousands of immigrants made their way to what they hoped were certain fortunes. In west Texas, the San Antonio-El Paso Road opened in 1849. It not only served as a passageway for the pioneers, it also carried hundreds of freight trains carting badly needed goods to the new settlers. Ten years later, when the Butterfield Overland Express commenced operations, the El Paso Road became an important link in the route that led mail coaches from St. Louis to San Francisco.

These important thoroughfares passed directly through territory used by Apache and Comanche warriors. By the time of the great westward expansion in the late 1840s and early 1850s, raiders from these tribes had already wiped out the isolated villages and ranches of northern Mexico and southwestern Texas. It was inevitable that the warriors would prey on travelers traversing the El Paso Road. By

1854, the situation had grown so serious that the military decided to build a fort in west Texas.

The site chosen by Maj. Persifor F. Smith, commander of the army's Department of Texas, was in an area then called the Apache Mountains. Located at the mouth of a box canyon near Limpia Creek, this site offered ample quantities of wood, water, and grass for grazing animals. The new post was named Fort Davis in honor of Secretary of War (later President of the Southern Confederacy) Jefferson Davis. The Apache Mountains soon became known as the Davis Mountains.

Six companies of the Eighth U.S. Infantry were sent to garrison the fort. Their commander, Lt. Col. Washington Seawell, vehemently disapproved of the site because Indians could (and did) come very close without being spotted. Seawell obeyed orders, however, and placed the fort where he had been ordered to do so. It was a ragged

collection of more than 60 pineslab structures that were assembled in irregular fashion up the canyon. Seawell had a dream of someday building a fine stone fort on the open plain at the mouth of the canyon. This first fort, he felt, was a temporary measure.

He was wrong. Seawell spent most of the next seven years as commander of Fort Davis, which eventually did grow to include six stone barracks laid out in a line across the mouth of the canyon. But in the meantime officers continued to live in rotting log huts, and supplies fell to ruin in shabby warehouses roofed with canvas or thatched with grass. The men spent much of their time escorting the mail and freight trains, chasing (but rarely catching) raiders who had attacked travelers, and patrolling their sectors without ever really dealing with the Apache or Comanche. By the end of the decade, little had been done to solve the Indian problem.

With the advent of the Civil War, the frontier defense system of west

The fort's officers' quarters consisted of 13 large, single-unit dwellings for families and four multi-unit quarters for bachelors. One of the latter is seen here.

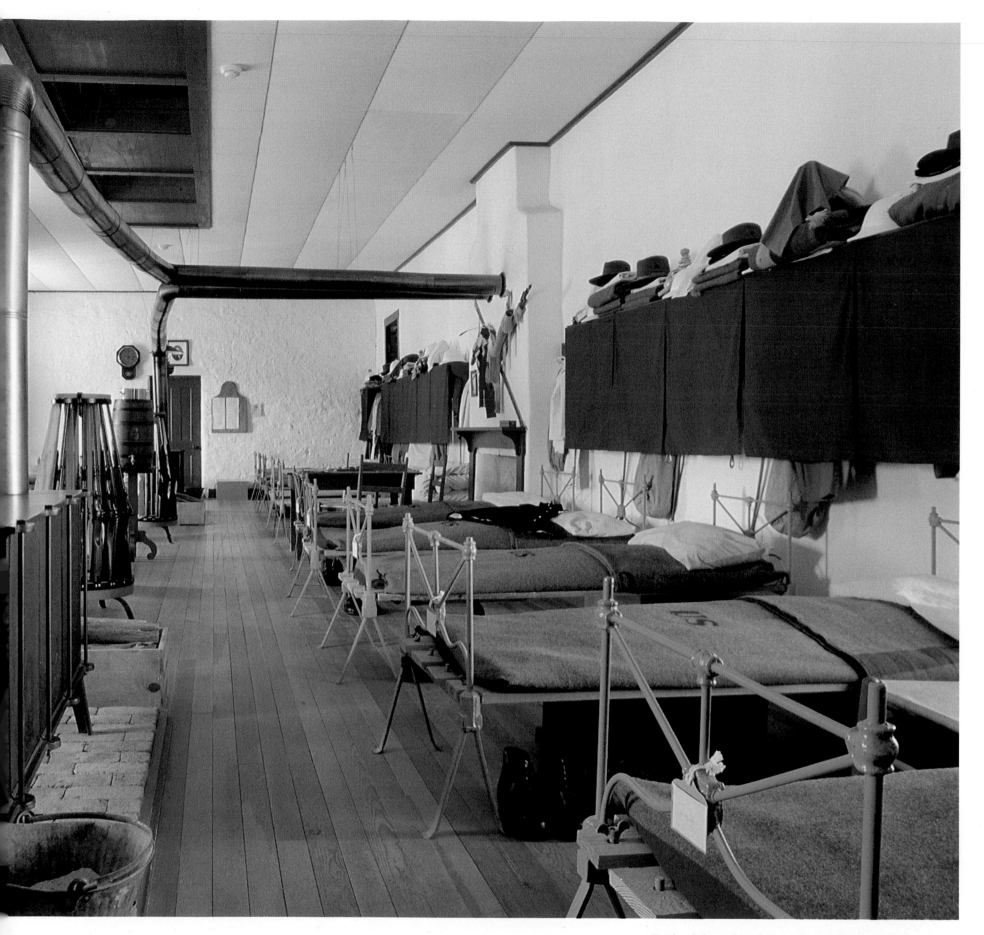

Each of the enlisted men's barracks at Fort Davis was built to house one company. In addition to the living quarters seen here, each of the adobe structures had a kitchen and a mess hall.

(above) The ruins of the hospital at Fort Davis. Built in 1875, it included a ward for 12 patients, although it often had to accommodate more. Another ward was built ten years later.

(right) Members of the Ninth U.S. Cavalry at Fort Davis pratice dismount drill around 1875.

Texas fell apart. When the state seceded from the Union in 1861, department commander for the United States, Brig. Gen. David E. Twiggs, ordered Fort Davis and its sister forts abandoned. Confederate troops occupied them in June 1861, thinking that they had friendly relations with the Apache in the area, but in August 1861, some of the Indians stole cattle and horses from the fort. When 14 soldiers pursued them, they were trapped and killed.

In spring 1862, Confederate troops evacuated the fort. Thereafter, Apache sacked the post, which then lay deserted for five years. In 1867, federal troops returned, among them the Ninth U.S. Cavalry, a newly organized African-American regiment. On the plain outside the canyon, commander Lt. Col. Wesley Merritt began to lay out and construct the fort that Seawell had dreamed of long ago. The first buildings were stone, but economics dictated a change to adobe. Completed in the 1880s, the new post consisted of quarters for 12 companies with more than 50 structures in total.

From 1867 to 1885, Fort Davis played host to African-American troops, commanded by white officers, among the first posts in the West to do so. Earning the respect of their Indian enemies, who dubbed them "Buffalo Soldiers," these troopers were instrumental in the Indian Wars, helping to end the conflicts with the Apache in 1886.

By 1891, Fort Davis outlived its usefulness and was abandoned by the army. Today the post lies on the northern edge of the town of Fort Davis, Texas. Half of the original structures have been restored. The Visitors Center and museum offers an audio program and slide show, and self-guided tours of the grounds are available.

Henry Flipper

Henry Ossian Flipper, born in Thomasville, Georgia, in 1856, came of age at a time in American history when dramatic social change marked the nation. In the post-Civil War era, newly freed blacks struggled for recognition and equality. But they didn't have an easy time of it, as whites in the South used "Jim Crow" laws and the intimidation of the Ku Klux Klan to keep African-Americans second-class citizens.

But Henry Flipper's parents were determined to see their children lead the best possible lives. They moved to Atlanta during Henry's childhood and, while his father worked as a shoe cobbler, the five Flipper sons received private tutoring. Henry's tutor was an ex-Confederate soldier trying to earn a living in the aftermath of the Civil War. All of the children went on to

Henry Flipper, the first African-American graduate of West Point.

good careers, one as a bishop, another as a doctor, and two as educators.

Henry Flipper was fiercely ambitious. This character trait—and a supportive Republican congressman, Georgia's first—enabled him to win an appointment to the U.S. Military Academy in June 1873. Four years later, he became the first African-American to graduate from West Point. Posted to Fort Davis, Texas, as Acting Commissary of Subsistence, the second lieutenant became a genuine anomaly among the black troops on the Western frontier—an African-American officer in an army which saw even all-black units commanded by whites.

But Flipper's military glory days were short. In summer 1881, he was accused of embezzling government funds and given a general court-martial. Although he was cleared of the charges, he was found guilty of conduct unbecoming an officer and dismissed from the service.

Refusing to let the humiliation destroy him, Flipper went on to lead an extraordinary life. He became a surveyor with an American land company in Mexico, opening his own Arizona engineering firm in 1890. At the end of the decade, he became the editor of the state's *Nogales Sunday Herald*. In 1919, he served as translator and interpreter for the Senate subcommittee on Mexican affairs, and then became assistant secretary of the Interior. Despite his successes, Flipper persisted unsuccessfully throughout his life to win a reversal of his court-martial. He died at 84 in 1940. In 1976, the army reviewed the court-martial transcripts and changed Flipper's discharge to an honorable one.

Lt. Col. Washington Seawell spent almost seven years as commander of Fort Davis, starting in 1854. His dream of a fine stone fort on the open plain ultimately came true, but long after he had departed.

(above) This photo, taken from the overlook on Sleeping Lion Mountain, provides a view of the barracks. The twin, T-shaped buildings were begun late in 1867 and occupied by 1869. The men lived in huts and tents during the construction.

(left) The sergeant who worked here would have been responsible for running the day-to-day operations of the commissary, including the issuing of rations and the ordering of goods. Several junior enlisted men serving as clerks would have reported to him.

(opposite) This costumed interpreter wears the uniform of a cavalryman of the 1880s, including the kind of fatigue hat that was worn on campaign. The fort was never attacked during its distinguished history.

FORT SELDEN

(*above*) The administration building, seen here in ruins, was on the east side of Fort Selden's parade ground. It housed the post storerooms, offices, and workshops. The guardhouse and jail cells were in the center of the structure.

(*opposite*) A lonely American flag flaps in the wind high above the ruins of Selden's barracks. Completed in January 1867, the fort initially housed 149 men and 6 officers.

While the Civil War raged, Native American tribes in New Mexico took advantage of the situation by conducting a violent campaign against white settlements. With the army otherwise occupied, they were soon able to destroy almost half of the small frontier enclaves in the southern portion of the territory. By the time the war ended, the army realized that a strong military presence was needed in the area to regain control. A fort would be built to serve two needs. First, it would protect settlers; and second, it would provide a way station that would lessen the dangers of traversing the huge expanse of desert known as Jornado del Muerto or the Journey of Death.

Fort Selden was built in 1865 on the banks of the Rio Grande, 18 miles north of the southern tip of the desert. The location was on a mesa flat, at a point in the river teeming with beaver and alive with cottonwood trees, and with good grazing land northeast of the site. The area appropriated for the fort was a square extending two miles in each of the four directions from a point on the parade ground. Thus, it contained 16 square miles.

The fort was named for Col. Henry Selden, an army veteran who saw action in the battles of Vera Cruz and Mon-

141

Buffalo Soldiers

At the end of the Civil War, freed slaves were suddenly faced with the need to earn a living. Aside from farming, few career possibilities presented themselves to the majority of the men. Some of them looked West—to become, among other things, cowboys or soldiers. In 1866, Congress created four African-American regiments, two cavalry units and two infantry units, to replace disbanding regiments of western volunteers and to man the new adobe forts being erected in the southwest.

The African-American regiments quickly won renown: they fought hard and often, had a lower desertion rate than did many white troops, and managed to maintain their morale and discipline during winter marches when many other soldiers despaired. Still, they faced enormous prejudice. They were cordoned into their own units, kept separate from the rest of the army, and invariably led by white officers, who more often than not treated the assignments as a form of punishment or exile.

It was the Indians who accorded the African-Americans a high degree of respect. They called them "Buffalo Soldiers," reflecting the resemblance Native Americans saw between the black soldiers' hair and the buffalo's shaggy coat. Since the buffalo was a sacred animal to the Indians, they considered the appellation an honor.

The African-American troops served widely. Fort Selden in New Mexico, for example, was garrisoned by black troops through one third of its existence. At Arizona's Fort Huachuca, members of the African-American Ninth and Tenth Cavalry were assigned to duty in the early 1900s. In 1916, some of their number joined Gen. John Pershing on his punitive expedition into Mexico. Until 1947, when segregated army units were abolished, Huachuca served as the national center for the Buffalo Soldiers.

terey in the Mexican War, during the War Between the States, and at the Battle of Valverde in New Mexico. He died two-and-a-half months prior to the start of the post's construction.

On April 15, 1865, troops were ordered from Fort Albuquerque to the site to begin work. The task of building the new outpost was initially given to the men from Company C, First Veteran Infantry California Volunteers, and from Company F, First Infantry New Mexico Volunteers. They were soon joined by another company of the California Column, bringing the total garrison to 149 men and six officers. Civilian employees and military prisoners assisted the troopers in the construction effort.

The post was a rough piece of work, consisting of flat, adobe buildings that were subject to deterioration. Decay was a constant problem throughout the fort's history. The administration building was a long, two-story structure housing the post storerooms, officers, and workshops. All of the men and officers had to endure dirt floors in their quarters until 1870, when most of the post was floored. The basic fort, however, was finished by January 1867.

Frontier posts like Fort Selden, with their almost primitive design, provided soldiers with a life that was primarily monotonous and often harsh. The nearest town of any interest was a rough place called Leasburg, which was quickly put off-limits. So those who could traveled the 12 miles to Dona Ana. It may have lacked Leasburg's excitement but at least it was a town. It didn't, however, have a railroad station. For that a soldier had to go all the way to Colorado, 549 miles to the north.

Post rations didn't make life at Fort Selden any easier. Fresh produce was not often available and on at least one occasion the flour was condemned as bug-ridden. Desertion was a constant problem, as men suffered from poor living conditions, isolation, and boredom.

Those who stayed saw little action. Selden's primary enemies were the

Apache, who proved to be an elusive lot. Still, any supply train, officer, or group of civilians passing through the area required a heavy escort. In order to provide better protection, picket posts were set up in two of the region's most troubled spots. They worked, but the Apache were not defeated. The bold tribe continued its raids, actually making off with the post quartermaster's herd of cattle on one occasion. They were caught.

In the entire 25-year history of the fort as an active outpost, only three men were lost in actual combat with the enemy. Twice as many men died in Selden's first 18 months of operation due to brawls in Leasburg.

To the regret of few, the fort was abandoned in July 1878, as the threat from Indians appeared to have waned. But Selden was reactivated in the 1880s with the arrival of the rail line. Buildings were repaired and reconstructed, a process completed by 1885, but the post never regained its two-company capacity. Many of the structures were simply too damaged to be

repaired. Among the fort's occupants during its second life was Capt. Arthur MacArthur, commander of Company K, 13th Infantry, traveling with his wife and sons, Arthur and Douglas. They remained for two years. Douglas, of course, went on to become a five star general, perhaps the most celebrated American commander of the 20th century. Expansion of the fort was discussed for years, as a permanent 12-company post was needed in the area. With the

development of the towns of El Paso and San Antonio, in Texas, however, it became clear that Fort Selden had outlived its usefulness. Both towns were major railroad centers, and the monies that had been allocated to expand the fort were given to Fort Bliss, closer to El Paso. The final abandonment of Fort Selden began in 1887 and ended in 1891. The fort is now a New Mexico State Monument.

Among those who served at Fort Selden during the 1880s was Capt. Arthur MacArthur, seen here with his wife Mary and his sons. The younger boy, Douglas (left), grew up to become one of America's most celebrated military leaders.

A costumed interpreter engages in target practice beside the ruins of the fort's hospital. During Selden's heyday, the garrison had little opportunity to employ its skill with firearms. Indeed, in the fort's 25-year history as an active outpost, only three men were lost in actual combat with the enemy.

(*above*) This two-story wooden barracks, built in 1823, played host to a wide variety of units over the years, including the Tenth Cavalry, an African-American unit which joined in the pursuit of Pancho Villa in 1916.

(*opposite*) A trooper scrapes and cleans his horse's hoofs. For a cavalryman on a remote outpost during the 19th century, such a skill was imperative.

The area of southeastern Arizona that forms the setting for Fort Huachuca has been inhabited since at least 11,000 B.C. Mammoth remains have been found on a ranch near the town of Hereford, along with projectile points probably used to spear the animals. It has also been established that as early as the year 1400 A.D., a thriving Native American population was making its home in the canyons of this mountainous area.

The name Huachuca, which is applied to the nearby mountain range as well as the fort, came from a later Indian tribe, who used it to describe its home. The word is usually translated as "place of thunder," an apt description of the area in summer months. It has also been said to mean "place of wind and rain," two other distinct characteristics of the site.

The actual fort was built during the Indian Wars that raged throughout the West in the 1870s and 1880s. In February 1877, Col. August Kautz, commander of the Department of Arizona, ordered Capt. Samuel Marmaduke Whitside to take two companies of the Sixth Cavalry and establish a temporary camp in the Huachuca Mountains.

The old headquarters building, built of adobe in 1917, still serves as the post headquarters today.

Its purpose was to protect settlers and their travel routes in southeastern Arizona while also intercepting Indian raiders.

On March 3, 1877, Captain Whitside selected a location in the canyons, one that provided fresh running water, plenty of trees, an excellent view in three directions, and protective high ground, all essentials for security against the Apache. Moreover, the location of the fort in the San Pedro Valley blocked the tribe's traditional escape routes to Mexico.

In 1886, members of Fort Huachuca's B Troop, Fourth Cavalry Regiment, were chosen to pursue the renegade Apache Geronimo. The fort was to be the advance headquarters and forward supply base for what was expected to be a hard-fought campaign. Fort Bowie, with more efficient rail, road, and telegraph communications, served as the rear base. For five months, the fort's troops pursued the fugitive Apache, covering more than 3,000 miles, before bringing him to bay. Geronimo's surrender in August 1886 virtually ended the threat of organized Indian attacks in southeast Arizona. Thus, the army closed more than 50 camps and forts in the region, but Fort Huachuca was kept open, primarily because of continuing border trouble with renegade Indians, Mexican bandits, and American outlaws.

In 1913, the Tenth Cavalry arrived. These African-American soldiers were to remain on the post for almost 20 years. In 1916, the unit temporarily departed to help track down Pancho Villa during Gen. John J. Pershing's punitive expedition. It was an unsuccessful campaign but the Tenth performed well. Huachuca again served the Tenth Cavalry during World War I, when its principal role was guarding the Arizona-Mexico border.

By 1933, the Tenth Cavalry had been replaced by the 25th Infantry Regiment as the main combat unit at the fort. In turn, the 25th was absorbed by the 93rd Infantry Division during World War II. When the 93rd left for the Pacific in 1943, the 92nd Infantry Division arrived for training and subse-

Geronimo

An Apache of the Mimbres band, Geronimo was born in 1829 in present-day Clinton, Oklahoma, and given the name Gokhlayeh (One Who Yawns). His father had been a chief but had forfeited his leadership role by marrying into a different tribe. Gokhlayeh knew that his only chance for prestige was as a warrior.

He had the physique of a fighter. He also had the temperament, possessed of ample helpings of cunning and toughness. His famous ferocity can be traced to 1858, when his tribe decided to accept the invitation of the Mexican government to attend a peace conference in nearby Chihuahua. Gokhlayeh traveled to the town with the delegates of his tribe, accompanied by his wife, their three young children, and his mother. When they arrived in Chihuahua, they found they had been deceived. The Mexicans attacked the Apache, killing or imprisoning most of them. The warrior survived. His family did not.

After that, Gokhlayeh's lust for Mexicans became obsessive. Two years later, he attacked the town of Arizpe in Sonora, killing like one gone mad. One Mexican watching him was compelled to shout "Geronimo!"—Jerome, in Spanish—and the nickname was taken up by Indians and Mexicans alike.

That battle marked the beginning of the Apache warrior's formidable

reputation. Thereafter, he was involved in numerous border wars against white settlers, plunging the Arizona region into bloodshed and fear. His eagerness to fight soon drew the attention of the United States Army, which undertook a lengthy campaign to kill or capture him. He did in fact surrender once, in 1884, only to take flight again a year later, accompanied by 40 men and about 90 women and children. The chase to capture the wily Apache grew desperate, but Geronimo, well armed and brutal, proved almost impossible to run to ground. Finally, in 1886, when he was about 57, he surrendered for the second time to the authorities. The manhunt that led to his capture involved some 5,000 troops. Geronimo had merely 38 Apache followers. He lived for 23 years after his surrender, exiled to Florida and later Oklahoma.

Geronimo (right) in a photo dated 1886, the year in which the fierce Mibres Apache warrior surrendered for the second and final time.

In 1913 the Tenth Cavalry arrived at Fort Huachuca. These African-American soldiers—nicknamed "Buffalo Soldiers" by the Indians—were to remain on the post for almost 20 years.

The maneuvers, uniforms, and equipment used by members of B Troop today are authentic reproductions of those used by the unit when it protected settlers from Indians and Mexican banditos during the last decades of the 19th century.

B Troop members use 1904-model McClelland saddles. Their sidearms are .45-calibre colt revolvers and their rifles are Springfield carbines, shorter than the average rifle and therefore better suited to the needs of a mounted soldier.

quent European assignment. During the war years, troop strength at the fort reached 30,000 although the post could really only accommodate about a third of that number. Finally, at the end of World War II, the fort was deactivated and transferred to the state of Arizona. It was reactivated by army engineers during the Korean War and, following that conflict, became the home of the army's Electronic Proving Ground. In 1967, the headquarters for what is now known as the Information Systems Command was moved there, and two years later, the post became the home of the Army Intelligence Center and School. It is the only active army post left in Arizona dating from the 1800s out of the more than 70 created during that time.

In 1960, the Fort Huachuca Historical Museum was established on the site to inform the public about the southwest's colorful military history. It is located at the mouth of Huachuca Canyon on "Old Post," an area featuring most of the original buildings constructed in the 1890s. The museum annex, the newest addition, has a recreation of a frontier town set around a natural wildlife display involving animals native to the area.

(below) **Capt. Samuel Marmaduke Whitside established Camp Huachucha on March 3, 1877.**

(top) **During the 1880s, troopers from Fort Huachuca participated in the campaign to track down Geronimo. There were probably about 150 men stationed on the post at the time.**

(above) **Troopers demonstrate the use of field artillery at Fort Huachuca but in the Old West cannon was rarely carried by cavalry units. They were too cumbersome to transport over the rugged terrain.**

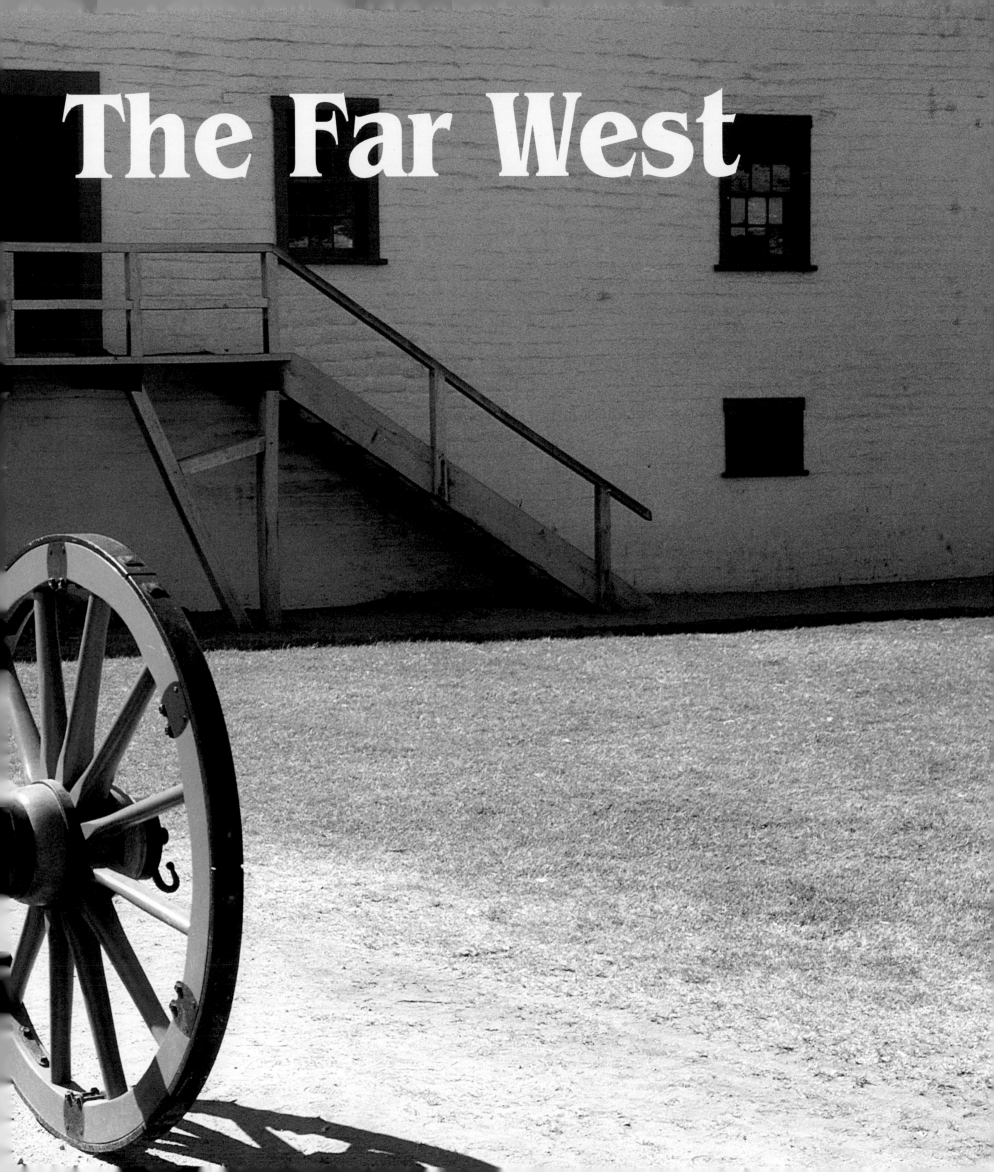

The Far West

(above) Most of Fort Cove was constructed from the surrounding area's black volcanic rock and dark limestone. The walls were 100 feet long and 18 feet high.

(opposite) The rear entrance to Fort Cove gives some sense of the walls' thickness—which ranges from four feet at the foundation to two feet at the top. In addition to serving a defensive role, the post was a communications and transportation hub within the Mormon Corridor.

(previous pages) Sutter's Fort, established in 1841, near present day Sacramento, California.

In 1847, when Mormon pioneers began arriving in what would later become Utah Territory, they settled in the valleys and flatlands. Under the guidance of their spiritual leader, Brigham Young, these settlers quickly make their presence known. By the time Young died in 1877, the Church of Jesus Christ Of Latter-day Saints—as the Mormons are officially called—had founded nearly 400 communities in what is now Utah, Idaho, Wyoming, Nevada, Arizona, California, and New Mexico. Each settlement was intended to be a separate place where church members could practice their religion without the harassment they had known back East.

An area of concentrated settlement fell along the western slopes of the Wasatch range of mountains from Brigham City, Utah, on the north to San Bernadino, California, on the south. This line of relatively dense population became known as the "Mormon Corridor" and was a crucial factor in transportation, communication, and defense among church communities along the western frontier. Cove Fort was part of this corridor, constructed to help Mormon pioneers, many of whom had recently arrived from as far away as England and Scandinavia. Not only did

Brigham Young

The early history of the Church of Jesus Christ of Latter-day Saints is a violent one. The sect was formed in 1830 by Joseph Smith, a young farmhand from upper New York State. His group was driven from Ohio to Jackson County in western Missouri, where it established roots. Relations with the neighbors were unfriendly, however, due to the Mormons' abolitionist beliefs and, eventually, due to Smith's espousal of polygamy. The group fled again to Illinois, where Smith was killed by a mob in 1844.

The sect threatened to dissolve after Smith's death. Its savior was Brigham Young, a 43-year-old church elder, who took over as Mormon leader. Born in 1801 in Whitingham, Vermont, Young had been employed as a painter and glazier in New York when he became attracted to the new Mormon religion. He was baptized in 1832 and, by 1835, had become one of the sect's cornerstones, traveling even to England, where he converted large numbers to his faith. Two years after he became the dominant figure in Mormonism, he led his believers West to establish their colony in the desert. Thereafter, he became director of the settlement that arose around the Great Salt Lake.

Young was an able statesman, a leader who was responsible for the growth and stability of the church and the community surrounding it. He was perhaps less adept as a military figure. In 1858, following the brief so-called Utah War between the State of Deseret—as Young's colony was called—and the U.S. Army, the government in Washington stripped Young and his followers of their state's independent status and removed Young from his governership. In his old age, the Mormon elder was brought up on charges of polygamy and murder but was acquitted. He died in 1877, leaving behind 17 widows (of the 27 women that he married during his lifetime).

Brigham Young became the Mormon's leader in 1844, following the death of the sect's founder, Joseph Smith.

these early settlers have to grapple with the harsh living conditions of the untamed West, they also had to adjust to differences in climate and culture.

Cove Fort was located between Fillmore and Beaver, two already established towns. In 1867, Brigham Young asked Ira Nathaniel Hinckley and his family to direct the construction of the outpost and to manage it upon its completion. The majority of the post was built between April and November, 1867. Workers came from nearby Mormon settlements and, for their efforts, received credits towards their tithes, the fixed percentage of earnings or possessions that each congregant was expected to give to the church. Most of the fort was constructed from the area's black volcanic rock and dark limestone. The walls were 100 feet long, 18 feet high, and varied in width from four feet at the foundation to two feet at the top. In total, the structure consumed nearly 2,000 cubic yards of stone and 2,000 bushels of lime.

Wood—primarily cedar and pine taken from the surrounding woods—was used abundantly in the fort's interior. Indeed, more than 34,000 board feet of lumber were employed for the interior rooms, shingles, roof trusses, catwalks, runways, and decorative moldings, as well as for the massive doors built at the east and west ends of the fort. The post featured 12 rooms which were used for a variety of domestic and social activities. The half dozen rooms on the north bank provided living quarters for both permanent and temporary residents. The other six, on the south bank, served as a post office, arsenal, dining room, telegraph office, pantry, cellar, washroom, and kitchen. In the courtyard was a cistern and a hydrant through which a small branch of Cove Creek ran.

Among the largest structures on the site was the barn, 60 feet by 60 feet, with a center portion that stretched 30 feet high. It had two levels for the storage of both hay and grain. There was also room for the horses of the Hinckley family and those of other travelers and visitors. The stockade was attached to the barn and measured 150 feet by 200 feet. The Mormons also built a racetrack on the site, a half-track that allowed them to engage in a favorite recreation. Despite their penchant for

This impressive facade gives entrance to Fort Cove, one of a number of Mormon outposts that were created in Utah during the 1860s to serve the sect's pioneers.

horse racing, the fort's residents spent a great deal of time at work—ranching, farming, and caring for the many travelers who passed through the region. These included not only other Latter-day Saints on their way to new homes, but also church leaders, mail carriers, explorers, tourists, and businessmen. All were given food and lodging, and their animals were fed and stabled. Cove Fort was a relay station of the Deseret Telegraph, a system of communication constructed in 1866/67 to complement the transcontinental network completed in 1861. Shortly after the telegraph office began operating, a post office was established at the fort. Sulphur mining later became an important part of the region's existence, due to a rich supply in the area. Fort residents often worked in the mines, and cared for those arriving to perform similar jobs.

In 1903, when the fort's original functions were no longer required, it was leased by the church to William Kessler who renovated it and operated it as a hostelry. A store and gas station soon opened. In 1927, the 60th anniversary of the establishment of the fort was celebrated. Over the years, tourists have continued to visit this historic Mormon outpost and a preservation program was established. The directors of the site are presently engaged in a program (to be completed in the mid–1990s) that will completely restore the fort, outbuildings, and landscape.

(right) An old wagon wheel at Fort Cove serves as a reminder of the arduous journey endured by the Mormons in their search for religious freedom and a land of their own. The original band of pioneers, led by Brigham Young, arrived in Utah in 1847.

(below) In 1867, Brigham Young asked Ira Nathaniel Hinckley (left) and his family to direct the construction of Cove Fort and to manage the post upon its completion. With Hinckley in this photo is his brother, Arsa Erasmus Hinckley.

(left) The half dozen rooms on the fort's north bank provided living quarters for both permanent and temporary residents.

(below) Fort Cove featured 12 rooms which were used for a variety of domestic and social activities. In addition to living quarters, there was a post office, a telegraph office, and an arsenal.

(above) Eucalyptus trees frame one of Fort Ross' twin blockhouses, where artifacts and exhibits tell the story of Russia's experience at colonizing the New World.

(opposite) The small wooden Russian Orthodox chapel was built around 1824 but was rarely used, as the fort had no priest. The church was destroyed by fire in 1974 and authentically reconstructed.

In a wonderful, complex mix of culture and language, Fort Ross was founded in 1812 by 95 Russians and 40 native Alaskans who had come to California to hunt for sea otter, grow wheat and other crops for the Russian settlements in Alaska, and to trade with the Spanish settlers. Their hardy redwood fort now stands on the rugged Sonoma coast, once the most distant outpost of the Russian Empire.

The suggestion to colonize the northern California coast had initially been made in 1795 by Nikolai P. Rezanov, chief executive of the Russian American Company, who believed that an outpost there could become a valuable source of food supplies for Russia's settlements in Alaska and Siberia. He realized that although the Spanish claimed the land, they had no settlement there. Ivan Kuskov, assistant to the governor of Alaska, was in charge of building the fort and commanding its garrison.

As early as 1769, the fear of Russian expansion from Alaska had induced Spain to occupy Alta California. However, in 1812, San Francisco Bay marked the limit of Spanish settlement. During the summer of that year, as the fort was being built, the world's colonial powers were preoccupied with the Napoleonic War. It was several months before the Spanish Californians even realized that the construction of Fort Ross was underway.

By the end of the year, the walled enclosure with its two towers was complete. Ten structures would be built inside the walls in the coming years and, outside the fort, 50 assorted buildings were used by Russian workers, Aleuts, and Indians. Constructed with skill and an eye to detail, the one- and two-story buildings within the compound included the commandant's and official's quarters, barracks for employees, a kitchen, a warehouse, and a well-stocked armory. The latter, along with the many guards and the cannon displayed throughout the fort, gave a clear message to outsiders—the Russians were here to stay. However, in all of Fort Ross' days as a Russian outpost, there was never a single shot fired in anger.

By the mid–1830s, the Russian colony was besieged with problems. Over-hunting had severely depleted the area's stock of sea otter and other furs before the Russians even arrived. Worse, because of the colony's proximity to the sea and the damp, windy climate, Rezanov's plans for a thriving agricultural community never materialized. Trade with other Pacific countries had been a disappointment, too, thanks in large part to hearty competition from England and the United States. Mexico had begun to encourage foreign immigrants (especially Americans) to settle on the borders of the Russian colony to prevent it from expanding further. However, the Russians did have success raising cattle; their herd reached an impressive 2,000 head. Moreover, the colony established the first shipyard in California, at which three oceangoing vessels were constructed. Other boats and barges were built and sold to the Spanish Missions.

In 1839, the Russian experiment at colonizing what would become United States territory came to an end (with the exception of Alaska, which was not

The Aleuts

Somewhere in modern-day California there are people who have vestiges of Aleut blood in them, people who can trace their roots back to a historically important race of native Alaskans. Just how these people came to make their way to California is part of the wonder of the settlement of the West.

The Aleuts were closely related to the Eskimos, with similar languages and cultures. First "discovered" by Danish explorer and navigator Vitus Bering in 1741, they lived in relative obscurity until the arrival of the Russians a few decades later. With the settlement of Alaska by Russia came a new way of life for these indigenous people. Previously, they had had no concept of rank or privilege. The Russians created a political order, with chiefs to carry out various commands. Conscription was put into place and all males between the ages of 18 and 50 were liable for service to the Russian Empire, while women were used for domestic labor. If the newcomers' presence was bewildering and intrusive to the Aleuts, the Russians displayed a somewhat enlightened attitude toward the natives for that time and place. They paid their native workers, used them for only specified periods of time, and provided them with clothing and food.

The natives were most valued as hunters of sea otters and seals. They quickly exhausted the areas they had previously fished, attempting to meet the needs of the Russians, and it was not unusual to spot Alaskan Aleuts hunting as far south as the coast of San Diego.

When Fort Ross was colonized in 1812, 40 Russians and 80 Aleuts arrived to do the job. Indeed, the Aleuts in conjunction with the Kashaya, a local Native American tribe, built the fort.

The Aleutian Islands, a group extending southwest off Alaska, were named for these natives.

Aleuts in baidarkas, circa 1790.

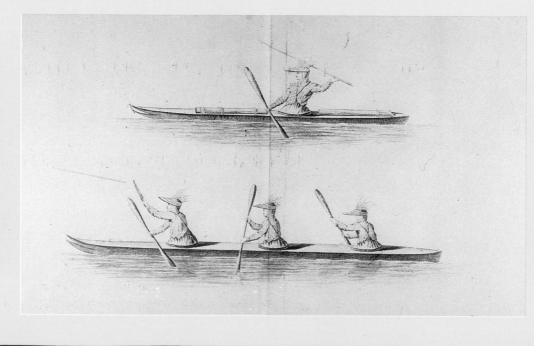

(*above*) Tall walls surround the compound at Fort Ross, with high gates sweeping open to give entrance to the parade ground. The commandant's house is visible in the center of this photo.

(*left*) In 1839, Alexander Rotchev, Fort Ross' final commandant, was given the task of selling the Russian outpost. He did so in 1841 to Capt. John Sutter for the sum of $30,000, but the money was never collected.

sold to the United States until 1867). Although the governor of Alaska tried to retain the outpost for Russia in exchange for recognition of the newly independent Mexico by Tsar Nicholas I, the tsar rejected the notion, and instead approved the sale of Fort Ross. Finding a buyer, however, proved to be a tough task. Alexander Rotchev, the final commandant of the fort, approached Britain's Hudson's Bay Company, the French government, and even Mexico. Finally he sold the property in 1841 to Capt. John Sutter,

whose colony New Helvetia was located near present-day Sacramento. Sutter agreed to pay $30,000, but the money was never collected.

Today, Fort Ross State Historic Park offers the most complete example of Russia's heritage in the United States. The commandant's house—once damaged by fire but now restored—is an impressive structure. The two blockhouses, the stockade, and the chapel have been carefully reconstructed to match the original buildings. The chapel is possibly the most interesting structure on the site, a small, wooden Russian Orthodox church that was used rarely as there was no priest at the fort.

(above) The modern museum at Sutter's Fort is located next to the reconstructed northwest bastion, seen at left in this photo.

(opposite) Sutter grew bountiful crops of grapes, which were then put to good use in his distillery, a forerunner of California's present wine industry.

John Augustus Sutter was a bit of a rogue, a man with a murky past that few would have been proud of. He rose to riches and fame, only to end his life in financial ruin. Born in 1803 to Swiss-German parents, he worked in the Swiss Canton of Berne, married, and opened a dry-goods shop. At the same time, he served as an officer in the Berne infantry reserve. He did well in business for a time, but as his family grew, his finances shrank. Finally, in 1834, Sutter fled his bad debts, abandoned his wife and five children, and set out to make his fortune in America.

He arrived in New York and promptly headed West. His first stop was Missouri, where he joined a trading caravan to Santa Fe, New Mexico. He later lost a business in Kansas, and traveled with the American Fur Company to the Rockies. From there, he made his way to the Hudson's Bay Company headquarters at Fort Vancouver. Sutter was eager to reach California. To get there, he set sail on a company ship to Hawaii in the fall of 1838 and journeyed three months later to Alaska. He finally reached Alta California in the fall of 1838.

Upon his arrival, Sutter was granted a passport to settle in what was then a Mexican province. He went to San

(above) The basis of John Augustus Sutter's empire was land. He received a grant of 47, 827 acres from the California colonial governor in 1841, having become a citizen of Mexico a year earlier.

(right) In the bakery, a costumed interpreter readies loaves of bread for the oven. Sutter planted grain on the grounds of the fort for use in making flour.

Francisco, playing the role of businessman, gentleman, and military officer. He visited all of the prominent local business leaders, presenting letters of introduction that he had obtained on his travels and establishing credit as he went. In August, he set sail on the Sacramento River with a flotilla of three vessels and a party of 18, bound for the province's central valley. Later that month, traveling the American River, his party landed about a mile from where Sutter's Fort stands today.

By 1841, construction of Sutter's outpost—made of adobe brick—was underway, and crops were being planted. The compound was 320 feet long, 150 feet wide, and contained a three-story central building that Sutter used as his headquarters. He greatly enjoyed playing the role of gentleman and host, welcoming those who came

The Forty-Niners

In 1848, a man by the name of Marshall was building a sawmill for a man named Sutter when he discovered a nugget of what soon proved to be gold. Word of the discovery, reported in the San Francisco papers in March, slowly made its way East. But no one seemed particularly excited about the event until President James K. Polk mentioned it in an address before Congress on December 5. Then gold fever struck with vengeance and life in California hasn't been the same since. The influx of people in one year alone—1849, the year of the gold rush—was estimated at between 60,000 and 100,000 people; before Marshall's discovery, the non-white population in all of Alte California had only been 14,000! And still they continued to pour in. By 1852, the population of the state (California entered the Union in 1850) had reached 223,856. About a fifth of that total had arrived by ship from Asia, Australia, South America, and western Europe. The rest came from other parts of America. And virtually all of them came for one thing—gold.

The first prospectors were amply rewarded for their labors, with one lump of gold found at Sonora weighing in at 28 pounds. Of course, nuggets of that size were rare but men working in Coloma, the site of the original find, managed to extract ore worth $25 to $30 a day. At the time, skilled labor elsewhere in California earned a mere $3.

But most of the Forty-Niners weren't so lucky. They started off poor, barely able to afford the basic tools of their new career—a mule, a pickax, a pan, and some food—and they stayed poor. The romance of prospecting was quickly replaced by a lot of dirty, hard, back-breaking work.

Fortune-seekers from everywhere—nicknamed Forty-Niners—came to try their luck in the California goldfields.

to help harvest grapes and wheat, to raise cattle, and to catch salmon. On August 29, 1840, he became a naturalized citizen of Mexico and, in September, was appointed Justice of the Peace and official representative of the government. A year later, Governor Alvarado gave Sutter a grant of 47,827 acres, and the entrepreneur named his empire New Helvetia. That same year, Sutter purchased Fort Ross from the Russians for $30,000, making a down payment of $2,000 and agreeing to pay the rest in crops and goods over the next few years. In 1844, he was appointed captain in the Mexican army and given the title Military Commander of the Northern Frontier. After helping quell a revolt against the government, he was awarded another 96,800 acres.

John Sutter was wealthier than he could have dreamed. His empire included 150,000 acres of land, herds of cattle, and shipping, tanning, and fishing industries. And then the dream began to dissolve. In 1846, his loyalties to the United States were considered suspect. While the Bear Flag Revolt against Mexico raged, the army put an American, Edward Kern, in temporary command of Sutter's Fort but the Swiss entrepreneur regained control of his outpost in 1847.

That year, he signed contracts with James Marshall to build on land leased from the Coloma Indians. On January 24, 1848, while working on a mill for Sutter, Marshall discovered gold. Despite Sutter's efforts, the discovery could not be kept secret, and soon the great California gold rush was on. By May, Sutter began to lose his workers to the gold fields. His crops went unharvested and chaos reigned as hordes of Forty-Niners overran his holdings. When his eldest son, John Jr., arrived from Switzerland, Sutter left his by-then heavily mortgaged property in the hands of his progeny and set off for Coloma. The beleaguered businessman had long planned to build Sutterville, a town that would be a tribute to his own greatness, on a plot of high ground, away from the river. In his absence, young John Augustus was convinced by his father's rivals that the town should be placed in a different location. Thus, when Sutter returned after his winter away, he discovered that the new community had been established between the fort and the river, and it was called Sacramento instead of the dreamed-of Sutterville. The rift between father and son grew, much to the advantage of every unscrupulous businessman in the area.

By 1849, Sutter was living on credit. He leased every room in Sutter's Fort and then sold the post outright for $7,000. By 1850, his wife and remaining children joined him in America. He gained recognition as a Major General with command of the California Militia, even as squatters began to overtake his land. In 1864, the state legislature voted Sutter a pension of $15,000, payable in monthly installments of $250. A year later, Sutter moved his family to Washington, D.C., bitter that he had not been given recompense from the federal government for his lost properties. He died of heart failure on June 18, 1880.

Reconstruction of Sutter's Fort began in 1891. Today, a visit is like a step back to 1846, with costumed interpreters re-creating the tasks of spinning, weaving, and drilling under the watchful eye of their host and protector, John Sutter.

(left) On January 24, 1848, while working on a mill for Sutter, James Marshall discovered nuggets in a stream bed and started the beginning of the greatest gold rush in U.S. history.

(below) The main gate at Sutter's Fort gives entrance to the adobe brick outpost established by the Swiss-German entrepreneur in 1841.

(above) Costumed interpreters demonstrate the art of open-air cooking, mastered by 19th-century pioneer women on the journey West. Their heavy clothing must have been cumbersome and hot during such labors.

(right) A "worker" slowly polishes his weapon inside the guardhouse. The fort did not come under siege until 1848, when squatters who came in search of gold began to settle on Sutter's land.

The fort's well—a vital fixture on any frontier outpost—was situated in front of the company headquarters, once the center of Sutter's vast empire.

A rough-and-ready group gathers on the grounds of the fort for a little impromptu music, a pleasant way of passing the time in a pioneer settlement.

(above) Fort Tejon was established in 1854 at a location known as Traveler's Rest. It featured ample building materials, grazing land was accessible, and the site was close to the sea coast so that supplies could be easily transported to and from it.

(opposite) This room in the barracks re-creates the occupancy by 1st Sargent William McCleave of Company K in 1857. He was a supply sergeant for his company, hence the array of goods.

In early 1853, the U.S. Army decided that Fort Miller in California's San Joaquin Valley had to be replaced. Established in mid-1851, the fort had become inadequate for the army's needs and was terribly expensive to maintain. Among other things, its isolation made shipping supplies to it very costly during the seven months that roads were passable. Moreover, the fort sat on private land. Its continued operation would have eventually required a settlement with the owners.

Still, a fort was needed in the area; law dictated that an army post had to be placed upon all newly created Indian reservations. Troops would police the Military Indian Reserves—as they were called—as well as act as buffers between the Native Americans and local whites. They were also to help teach the now pacified Indians animal husbandry and agricultural skills. The Sebastian Military Indian Reserve that had been established in what is now southern California required a post, and Fort Miller was not up to the job.

With this in mind, a dragoon company was transferred from Oregon to Fort Miller in spring 1854, while quarter-

One of the first buildings to be erected at the
fort was the enlisted men's barracks, whose
construction began in 1854. It is made of
adobe brick with a wood shingled roof.

master officers selected a site at the foot of Tejon Pass. Maj. James L. Donaldson, who was given the task of creating the new post, arrived at the site to find the army camp already installed. He passed along concerns from Indian Affairs that a military presence in the area was not needed but this viewpoint was considered merely political in nature, and ignored. If they were to stay, then in Donaldson's opinion, the site they had chosen was almost as undesirable as Fort Miller—it too would have incurred high freighting costs. The commander found a new site 17 miles away at a location known as Traveler's Rest. It featured ample building materials, grazing land was accessible, and the site was close to the sea coast so that supplies could be easily transported. Donaldson called the new post Camp Canada de las Uvas, but it soon assumed the name of its predecessor, Fort Tejon.

For six years, construction of the fort continued sporadically. The weather created delays, as did changes in governmental policy, financial crises, and occasional military activity. Most of the work was done by hired civilian labor. When it was finally completed, there were more than 40 military buildings on the site as well as two structures belonging to George Alexander, the post suttler. The fort served a number of roles during its numerous active years. Patrols from the post rode the supply route to and from Los Angeles and occasionally escorted travelers to Salt Lake City. The troopers guarded miners, chased bandits, and offered protection to most of the southern part of the state. Although their primary purpose was to protect the local Indians by serving as their police force, they also acted as enforcers of civil law when necessary and attempted to curtail the horse-stealing activities of the eastern desert tribes. In addition, the fort quickly became a military, social, and political hub for the area.

The dining room of this officer's quarters reflects the occupany of Captain Gardiner, commanding officer of Company A, from July 1855 to September 1856. For a frontier outpost of its day, this two-story structure represented a very high standard of living.

(above) In 1866, two years after Fort Tejon was abandoned by the army, it became part of a large ranch owned by Edward F. Beale.

(opposite) A "private," wearing a dress frock coat and Albert cap, circa the 1850s, relaxes in the general quarters of the enlisted men's barracks.

In June 1861, two months after the firing on Fort Sumter in Charleston Harbor, South Carolina, news of the outbreak of the Civil War reached California, and the post was abandoned. The civilian town of Fort Tejon died with the post. After its closure, the fort passed into the hands of an S. A. Bishop, who used the structures but did not maintain them. The army reoccupied the post in summer 1863 and remained until Tejon's final abandonment on September 11, 1864. In 1866, the fort became part of a large ranch owned by Edward F. Beale.

In 1916, a group of local citizens decided to bolster the walls of the four remaining original buildings. Not much more was done in the way of restoration until 1940, when five acres of land were donated to the California Division of Beaches and Parks. After World War II, 200 more acres were acquired and the buildings of Fort Tejon were reconstructed as part of Fort Tejon State Historic Park. The edifices are primarily adobe or wood-framed and represent the buildings of the post during its heyday.

Indian Reservations

During the late 18th and early 19th centuries, most Americans decided that peaceful co-existence with the Indians was simply not going to work. The best solution, they believed, was to divide the country up, reserving part of it for the various tribes and the rest for the people of the United States.

But what was life for the Indians to be like on those lands reserved for them? To answer that question, Congress passed a series of laws between 1790 and 1834. Known as the Indian Trade and Intercourse Acts, these statutes, in effect, treated reservation-bound Indians as separate nations, allowing them to be subject to their own laws rather than those of the United States. Agents appointed by the president served as liaisons between the federal government and the tribes, dispensing provisions, arresting liquor traffickers, evicting trespassers, and arranging periodic consultations between tribal chiefs and government representatives. The Acts also called for the hiring of teachers, carpenters, blacksmiths, and farmers who were to work under the agents and help move the Indians toward "civilization." Government trading houses were also introduced; Congress used $150,000 to stock reservation establishments that would compete with those of corrupt private individuals who had cheated the Indians while selling them domestic goods.

The lofty ideals that Congress had in mind when it enacted the Indian Trade and Intercourse Acts simply didn't come to fruition. To begin with, the natives did not want to be on the reservations. Asking them to accept new ways of life—new modes of living, new occupations, a new religion—only made matters worse. The Plains Indians, for example, were proud fighters. The placid, demanding life of a farmer simply didn't suit their temperament. Worse, giving the Indians handouts of food and other provisions often stripped them of any incentive to work. But worst of all, the reservations offered the Indians no security. Time and again, the government broke its treaty obligations with the Indians, taking land from a tribe that it had vowed would be theirs in perpetuity. Thus, the government's conviction that the Native Americans could be turned into happy, prosperous farmers just never materialized. Instead, most reservations were filled with poverty, alcoholism, and general misery.

Indian commissioner Maj. James McLaughlin (center) with members of his staff and reservation Indians.

ACKNOWLEDGEMENTS

The producers of *Forts and Battlefields of the Old West* gratefully acknowledge the following individuals who assisted in the creation of this book:

Alaska Historical Library, India Spartz; Barker Texas History Center, The University of Texas at Austin, John Slate; British Columbia Archives and Records Service, Brian Young, Leni Hoover; Bent's Old Fort National Historic Site, Craig Moore, Douglas Keller, Donald Hill, Bill Gwaltney; Big Hole National Battlefield, Jock Whitworth; California History Center, De Anza College, Nicholas Rokitiansky; California State Library, Carol Gilbert; The Church of Jesus Christ of Latter-Day Saints, Museum of Church History and Art, Don Enders, Steve Olsen; Colorado Historical Society, Rebecca Lintz, Patrick Fraker; Custer Battlefield National Monument, Kitty Deernose, John Doerner; The Daughters of the Republic of Texas Library, Martha Utterback; Fort Bridger State Museum, Cecil Sanderson; Fort Clatsop National Memorial, Scott Eckberg, Kurt Johnson; Fort Davis National Historic Site, Mary Williams, Ian Williams; Fort Huachuca, Margaret Liebchen, Tim Eliss, Dave Hewitt; Fort Laramie National Historic Site, Steve Fullmer; Fort Meade Museum, Ralph P. Hackert; Bob Lee; Fort Nisqually, Melissa McGinnis; Fort Robinson State Park, Marge Rotherham, Tom Buecker; Fort Scott National Historic Site, Arnold Schofield, Dave Schafer; Fort Selden Sate Monument, Jose Guzman, Keith Wallis; Fort Tejon, Don Schmidt; Fort Totten, Vance Nelson; Fort Union Trading Post National Historic Site, Paul Hedren; Fort Vancouver National Historic Site, Susie Menard; Idaho State Historical Society, Larry Jones; Montana Historical Society, Rebecca Kohl; Nebraska State Historical Society, Martha Vestecka-Miller; Oregon Historical Society, Marilyn Finn; Presidio La Bahia, John Collins; Roy Lake State Park, Wendy Lewis; San Jacinto Museum of History, Larry Spasic; South Dakota State Historical Society, Laura Glum, Marvene Riis; The State Historical Society of North Dakota, Todd Strand; Sutter's Fort State Historic Park, Mike Tucker; Wyoming Department of Commerce, Parks and Cultural Resources, Museums Division, LaVaughn Bresnahan.

PHOTO CREDITS

All of the color photographs in this volume are courtesy of Lynn Radeka, except for the following: pp. 38-39, South Dakota Tourism; p. 129, The San Jacinto Museum of History, Houston, Texas; p. 131, Texas Department of Commerce/Tourism Division, photo by Richard Reynolds; p. 149 (bottom), Arizona Office of Tourism. The black and white photographs are courtesy of the following:

Alaska State Library, Alaska Purchase Centennial Collection 160

British Columbia Archives and Record Service 100, 102

California State Library 164, 165, 175

Colorado Historical Society 56, 58 (bottom)

The Church of Jesus Christ of Latter Day Saints, Museum of Church History and Art 154, 156

Custer Battlefield National Monument 26, 78, 79

Dallas Historical Society 124

The Daughters of the Republic of Texas Library 116, 118, 123

Fort Union Trading Post NHS 49, 52

Idaho Historical Society 92 (top)

Joslyn Art Museum, Omaha Nebraska 51

Library of Congress 33 (top), 96, 130

Library of Congress, courtesy of the South Dakota Historical Society 30

The General Douglas MacArthur Memorial 143

Montana State Historical Society 43 (left), 85

National Archives of Canada 64, 108

National Archives 22, 27, 31, 72 (right), 84

National Park Service, Fort Davis National Historic Site 136, 137, 138

National Park Service, Fort Scott National Historic Site 13, 14

Nebraska State Historical Society 23

Oregon Historical Society 97, 111

Public Affairs Office, Headquarters, Fort Huachuca, Arizona 147, 149

The Remington Museum 142

Nicholas Rokitiansky 161

South Dakota Department of Game, Fish & Parks 36, 37

The State Historical Society of North Dakota 45, 175

Wyoming State Museum 65, 72, 75, 91, 103

Established in 1834, Wyoming's Fort Laramie served for more than 50 years as a landmark and way station for trappers, traders, missionaries, emigrants, Pony Express riders, and miners.